10 Keys
to Unlock
the Christian
Life

COLIN S. SMITH

10 Keys to Unlock the Christian Life

MOODY PUBLISHERS
CHICAGO

ISBN: 0-8024-6556-0
EAN/ISBN-13: 978-0-8024-6556-6

Library of Congress Cataloging-in-Publication Data

Smith, Colin S., 1958-
    Ten keys to unlock the Christian life / Colin S. Smith.
        p. cm.
    Includes bibliographical references.
    ISBN-13: 978-0-8024-6556-6 (alk. paper)
    1. Christian life. I. Title.

BV4501.3.S64 2005
248.4–dc22

2004025799

1 3 5 7 9 10 8 6 4 2

Printed in the United States of America

To my pastor, Derek Prime,

with grateful thanks for

your encouragement and example

Contents

Introduction

Every year, millions of people make a commitment of faith in Jesus Christ, but many don't know how to take the next steps forward.

This book will give you an inside look at the realities of the Christian life and show you how to grow in your faith. We're going to take a journey through 1 Peter, where we will discover ten keys to unlock the Christian life. This short New Testament letter, printed on just four pages in my Bible, is packed full of practical encouragement showing us how to live as Christians. It is a manual of discipleship, taking us inside the experience of the Christian life.

This study is designed as a follow-up to *10 Keys for Unlocking the Bible,* which gives an overview of the whole Bible story. If you have read other books in the *Unlocking* series, you will know that there is great value in taking a high-altitude flight over the whole Bible. This book will get your feet on the ground and help you come to grips with the Christian life.

LEARN THE CHRISTIAN LIFE

Peter was among the first disciples of Jesus, and he knew the highs and lows of the Christian life from his own experience. He walked on water because his faith was so strong, and he nearly drowned because his faith was so weak. He confessed that Jesus is the Christ, and then he denied that he had ever known Him. Peter knew that following Jesus is not for the fainthearted, but he discovered the grace of God in his own life, and was moved by the Holy Spirit to write this letter showing us the path of following Jesus.

LEARN HOW TO
LEARN FROM THE BIBLE

This letter has always had a special place in my own life. My own pastor, Derek Prime, believed that the best way to equip new believers was to teach them 1 Peter. His reasoning was simple: First Peter covers all the key issues of the Christian life in one book, and in exploring this one letter, Christians will *learn how to learn* from the Bible.

I've often been frustrated with discipleship manuals that send you jumping around the Bible from a passage in Ephesians, through three verses in Proverbs, to a great insight from an obscure place in 2 Samuel! That's a very unnatural way to study the Bible, and it is very confusing to a new Christian. It gives the impression that the teacher knows a great deal about the Bible but leaves new believers feeling that they could never learn by themselves because they would not know where to look.

This book will take you step by step through one book of the Bible. By the end of this study, you will know 1 Peter, but more than that, you will have the confidence of knowing how to learn from other books of the Bible as you continue to grow in the Christian life.

LEARN WHAT GOD
WANTS YOU TO KNOW

Another great advantage of learning the basics of the Christian life from one book of the Bible is that God sets the agenda. Many discipleship manuals pick out the themes that their author thinks important. That can be helpful, but the obvious danger is that the curriculum is slanted by the prejudices of the author and limited by his or her blind spots.

If I was writing a foundations course for new Christians, I would include sessions on Bible reading, prayer, and witnessing; but I don't think I would have planned sessions on freedom, confidence, humility, or coping with suffering. God knows that we need to learn these things, and that is why the Holy Spirit moved Peter to include them in this remarkable letter. Our aim is to explore God's discipleship manual *unedited*. As you get inside this letter, it will get inside you and provide God-given direction for your life.

THE AUDIENCE

So let's end this introduction with a quick look at Peter's introduction to his own letter. Here's how he begins:

> *Peter, an apostle of Jesus Christ,*
>
> *To God's elect, strangers in the world, scattered throughout Pontus, Galatia, Cappadocia, Asia and Bithynia, who have been chosen according to the foreknowledge of God the Father, through the sanctifying work of the Spirit, for obedience to Jesus Christ and sprinkling by his blood:*
>
> *Grace and peace be yours in abundance. (1 PETER 1:1–2)*

If you are into e-mail, you probably have several screen names. They are all different ways of describing yourself. Peter begins his letter (he didn't have e-mail) by identifying his audience. He gives us five "screen names" for Christian believers. They are "God's elect," "strangers in the world," "chosen [by] God," "set apart [that's what *sanctified* means] for obedience to Jesus Christ," and "sprinkled by the blood of Christ."

These are the staggering truths about every believer in the Lord Jesus Christ. If you have come to faith in Jesus Christ, these things are true of you. It's mind-blowing. If you were to live for a thousand years, you would not be able to understand it. The new reality of who you are in Christ is bigger than you can comprehend. It is something for you to receive and rejoice in.

Stop for a moment to let this sink into your soul. You have been chosen by God. You live in this world, but you don't belong to it. You belong to Christ. God has called you to a new life of obedience to Jesus and He has put you in a position where you can do it. Your past is forgiven. You have peace with God. You live in the world of grace. Now, let's explore that world together.

DISCOVER...

. . . what it means to be born again.

. . . how you can know that your faith is authentic.

. . . why angels long to grasp what you experience.

1
New Birth
1 Peter 1:1–12

So you've become a Christian. You said a prayer. You made a commitment. But what actually happened? What caused you to make this commitment when you did? Is anything really different, and how can you know for sure?

Take a look at your watch. You can see the movement as the seconds tick. What you don't see is the complex activity of wheels or electrical impulses inside the watch that make this movement happen. That's what it's like when a person comes to faith in Jesus Christ. God has been at work behind the scenes, opening your mind, warming your heart, and breathing new life into your soul.

The Bible calls this inner transformation the new birth, and that's the first thing that Peter wants us to discover.

> *Praise be to the God and Father of our Lord Jesus Christ! In his great mercy he has given us **new birth** into a living hope through the resurrection of Jesus Christ from the dead. (1 PETER 1:3, emphasis added)*

There is often a great deal of confusion over what is meant by the phrase "born again." People ask, "Are you a born-again Christian?" as if this was one brand among many.

When the Bible says "you have been born again" (verse 23), it means that God has brought a deep change at the very center of your being. He has given you a new nature, which means that you have a new disposition, a new appetite, and new capacities.

YOUR NEW DISPOSITION

God created you with your own unique gifts, personality, temperament, and abilities, and it is important to understand that the new birth does not violate what God has made.

Shy sinners become shy Christians. Zany sinners become zany Christians. Cautious sinners become cautious Christians, and cool sinners become cool Christians! The new creation does not contradict the old creation. God does not reverse what He has already done.

The Holy Spirit will help you to gain control to master your own temperament. He will give you power to overcome the effects of sin in your personality—like pride, anger, or greed. But God will not override His own work. He redeems His work by giving *you* a new disposition.

That's what happened to Peter. Christ took this man with his flair and passion and moved him in a whole new direction. Thomas never had that flair or passion. He was a more introverted type, a thinker who liked asking questions more than launching initiatives. Peter and Thomas were completely different men before they met Christ. And after they met Christ, they were completely different Christians. God's purpose is to take the unique individuality that He has already created in you and move that in a new direction.

Some time ago I talked with a teenager who had found it difficult to make a commitment to Christ. When I asked her what was holding her back, she told me that she did not want to be like her Sunday school teacher. The teacher was a rather straitlaced older lady who dressed in a conservative manner and didn't look like she laughed a lot. She was a very fine Christian, but her personality, temperament, and style were totally different from the fun-loving teenage girl!

I was glad to have the opportunity of explaining to the girl that becoming a Christian did not mean becoming like the teacher. Her face lit up as she saw that God wanted to take her unique personality and move *her* in a new direction.

God never intended you to spend your life trying to be like somebody else. Every person reflects a unique angle of the glory of God. He has made us all in His image, and yet He has never made two of us exactly the same. In the new birth, God takes your unique individuality and gives you a new disposition so that *you* can begin to live for His glory. There is no other Christian in the world like you.

YOUR NEW APPETITE

Nature determines appetite, and when you are born again, God gives you a new appetite that reflects your new nature. Birds have an appetite for worms and slugs. Cats have an appetite for meow mix. I don't care for either of these diets because it is not in my nature.

The principle is simple. Cats have an appetite for what cats love. Birds have an appetite for what birds love. Sinners have an appetite for what sinners love. And those who have been born again through the resurrection of Jesus Christ have an appetite for what Christ loves.

This does not mean that old appetites that might lead you into sin disappear. We live this Christian life in the flesh, and so we often find ourselves drawn to things that displease God. But these are not the deepest longings of your heart. Through the new birth, God creates a new desire within you to know Him, to please Him, and to follow Him.

Many people turn away from Christianity because they think it is about imposing a set of rules on a person's life. Obviously this is not attractive, and thankfully it is not what being a Christian is all about. In the new birth God creates a deep longing in you to live a new kind of life, and real freedom is found when what you most desire turns out to be exactly what God commands.

YOUR NEW CAPACITY

Nature determines capacity as well as appetite. Dogs can't fly; it's not in their nature. Fish can't run; it's not in their nature. In the same way, sinners can't live in the presence of God or obey the laws of God, because it's not in their nature.

That used to be your position. But when you were born again, God's Spirit came to live in you, giving you not only the desire to live a new life but also the capacity.

If your faith rested on a decision or commitment that you made, the Christian life would be impossible. You would be in the same position as the people in the Old Testament who promised to obey all of God's commandments. They were utterly sincere in their intent, but completely naive about their ability. But you can live this Christian life because God's Spirit is within you. You have the power and the capacity to do all that God calls you to do.

The Christian life is lived from within. It is the growth and outworking of a miracle that has happened within your soul by the power of God's Spirit. He has brought you to a new birth. He has given you a new disposition with new appetites and a new capacity.

Some people have a hard time connecting with this truth because they cannot remember a time or place where they made a definite commitment of faith in Christ. It's important to remember that a person's salvation comes through faith in Christ, not through a precise or vivid recollection of when that faith was formed.

I can't recall anything about my natural birth, but that does not cause me to doubt that I exist! The evidence that I was born is that I am alive. It's the same with the new birth. The evidence that a person has been born again is that he or she is living the new life. You discover that you have a new disposition and a new appetite, and the wonderful explanation for these things that you begin to see in yourself is that you have been born again.

No wonder Peter says, "Praise be to the God and Father of our Lord Jesus Christ! He has given us new birth." Never underestimate the miracle of what God has done in bringing you to faith in Jesus Christ.

WHY YOU?

Have you ever wondered why God moved in *your* life to bring you to faith? After all, there are millions of people who have never come to faith in Christ. When I think about the fact that some of my neighbors, family, and friends have never experienced the new birth, it leaves me asking the question "Why me?"

The only answer to that question is the mercy of God. It is "in his great mercy" that you have been born again (verse 3). Birth is something that happens to you. You do not contribute to it. God did not breathe new life into you because you were a better person or more sincere or more worthy than your unbelieving neighbors or friends. If any of these things were the cause of God's work in you, then the credit for your salvation would ultimately belong to you.

But Peter makes it clear that this is never the case. The only explanation for the miracle of your new birth lies in the mercy of God. Stop and ponder that for a moment. It will leave you with a sense of awe and mystery and wonder.

The reason you see the glory of Jesus is because He has opened your eyes.

The reason you love Him is because He has opened your heart. The reason you want to follow Christ is because He has given you that desire. And the ultimate explanation of these things is not to be found in anything in you, but rather in God, whose great mercy has touched and changed your life. God has been merciful to you. Let that bring you to worship.

If you began reading with the idea that becoming a Christian was all about you making a decision or saying a prayer, I hope you can see that much more was going on behind the scenes. God is at work in your life. In His great mercy He has given you new birth.

YOUR LIVING HOPE
THROUGH THE RESURRECTION

This new birth brings you into "a living hope through the resurrection of Jesus Christ from the dead" (verse 3).

Notice that your hope flows directly from the resurrection of Jesus. That's important. Peter is not talking about the power of a more optimistic view of life. I've listened to motivational speakers tell large audiences to "think positive and be positive." That may be good psychology, but it has nothing to do with Christianity.

Your living hope is not a mind game in which you create your own reality by the power of positive thinking. Peter tells us that it is tied to the resurrection of Jesus. When Jesus rose from the dead, He broke the power of death, and through the new birth the living hope of His victory touches and embraces you.

God has brought you to share in the triumph of Jesus' resurrection. Death has no hold over Him, and death will have no hold over you. When the moment of your death comes, whether that be through illness, old age, or what we call an accident or disaster, it will be a translation out of your body into the immediate presence of Jesus. Try to take that in. It will help you to overcome fear and to live with confidence.

KEPT BY GOD'S POWER

You have been born again "into an inheritance that can never perish, spoil or fade—kept in heaven for you" (verse 4).

Your new birth has brought you into a new family. You are a child of God, and as a member of His family you have a share in the greatest of all inheritances. God will keep that inheritance for you until the day when Jesus Christ will come and gather the whole family together into the immediate presence of God.

It is a wonderful thing to know that God is keeping a place in heaven for you. The reservation is made. It has been paid for by the blood of Jesus. There is an inheritance with your name on it, and when you see it you will not be disappointed.

But God does more than keep an inheritance for you. He also keeps you for the inheritance. Through faith, you are "shielded by God's power until the coming of the salvation that is ready to be revealed in the last time" (verse 5).

I've met many Christians who believe that God has an inheritance for them in heaven, but they sometimes wonder if they will arrive in heaven to receive it. God wants you to know that your salvation does not depend on your ability to hold on to Christ but on Christ's ability to hold on to you. It does not depend on the strength of your hand but of His, and His hand is stronger than yours. That's the basis of Christian confidence or assurance.

Christ is keeping an inheritance for you, and He is keeping you for the inheritance. Try to picture the two outstretched hands of Christ. In the one, He holds an inheritance. In the other, He holds you. Both are safe in His hands, and when He comes, He will bring the two together, and the inheritance will be yours.

TRIALS THAT PROVE
YOUR FAITH IS AUTHENTIC

In this you greatly rejoice, though now for a little while you may have had to suffer grief in all kinds of trials. These have come so that your faith . . . may be proved genuine and may result in praise, glory and honor when Jesus Christ is revealed. (VERSES 6–7)

If you found an old painting that resembled a Rembrandt, you would want to know if it was authentic, and you would seize any opportunity to find out. This is why the *Antiques Roadshow* has been such a success on TV. Experts arrive in a city, and people bring their antiques, wanting to know what they might be worth.

Your faith is of far more value than a Rembrandt painting. Peter says your faith is "of greater worth than gold." Gold will eventually perish like every other created thing, but your faith, if it is genuine, will last for eternity.

But how can you know that your faith is authentic? How do you know that it is not a passing phase? Peter has the answer. When you suffer grief in all kinds of trials, you will have all the evidence you need that your faith is authentic. Here's why: If your faith were just a human decision or a passing phase, then as soon as you began to suffer, you would renounce your faith and turn away from God. Then you would spend the rest of your life either saying you could no longer believe in God or else smoldering in bitterness and resentment against Him.

I can think of several people like that. No doubt you can too. The big question is "Why isn't everybody like that?" All of us experience some share of suffering in this life, so why don't we all turn away in bitterness and resentment?

Thinking about the congregation of believers I am privileged to serve in Arlington Heights, I can picture people who are struggling with un-answered questions, disappointed hopes, and shattered dreams. I think of some who have lost loved ones, others who have suffered severe illness, violence, or some other personal catastrophe. *And yet they still believe! They still love Christ!*

There is only one explanation for this: Christian faith is a miracle. It is the seed of the life of God planted within your soul, and it is indestructible.

Think about a bulb being planted in the ground, and try to imagine the experience from the bulb's perspective. The gardener takes you in his loving hand and digs a hole specially shaped for you. He places you in that hole, which seems like a gentle cradle. You look up to the light of the open sky above. Life is good and you are filled with joy.

Then, suddenly, the same gardener who seemed so caring drops piles of dirt on top of you. He buries you, and you find yourself surrounded by darkness. You think your life is at an end, but actually this is the beginning of your growth.

Grief and loss can bring us into experiences of great darkness. But faith is a living seed. Like the bulb, it grows where it is planted, and the amazing thing is that the dirt piled up over it actually contributes to its growth.

Think about your own experience: You have faced significant trials. You live with many unanswered questions. You have put your trust in Jesus Christ, but there are times when you are unable to grasp what He is doing in your life. And yet, if you are a believer, what Peter says will be true of you: "Though you have not seen him, you love him" (verse 8). You still believe in Him! There can be no greater evidence of the authenticity of your faith than that.

Faith that has been proved genuine will result in "praise, glory and honor when Jesus Christ is revealed" (verse 7). One day God will review everything that has happened in your life, including the places where you chose to love Him and trust Him through things that you did not understand. Then it will become clear that the darkest passages of your life were the places of your greatest triumphs. You will enter into the presence of Jesus with great joy and discover there the full value of your new life in Christ.

RECEIVING WHAT
OTHERS HAVE LONGED FOR

Peter concludes this marvelous opening section of his letter by reminding us of the immense privilege of this new life.

> *Concerning this salvation, the prophets, who spoke of the grace that was to come to you, searched intently and with the greatest care, trying to find out the time and circumstances to which the Spirit of Christ in them was pointing when he predicted the sufferings of Christ and the glories that would follow. (VERSES 10–11)*

The Old Testament prophets knew that God would send the promised Deliverer, and the Holy Spirit prompted them to speak about Him.

They knew that someone would come, that this person would suffer, and that afterward He would be surrounded with glory. But they did not know how this would happen or when He would appear.

The prophets longed to know more, and their whole lives were taken up with research as they carefully tried to discern how all this would come about. Their prophecies pointed forward to what you now experience through the new birth.

Think about it: You've got what Isaiah, Moses, and Elijah longed for. "They were not serving themselves but you, when they spoke of the things that have now been told you by those who have preached the gospel to you by the Holy Spirit sent from heaven" (verse 12).

Then Peter goes one fascinating step further: "Even angels," he writes, "long to look into these things." Angels enjoy life in the immediate presence of God, where they worship and serve their Creator. But since they have never sinned, they cannot know what it is to be forgiven. They do not share your experience of grace, and they cannot begin to imagine what it must be like for the Holy Spirit of God to live in you.

We may be intrigued by the experience of angels, but Peter tells us that angels are fascinated by our unique experience of God's grace. They long to look into these things. God's grace is more than angels can fathom. It leads them to worship, and it should do the same for you.

Can you see the breathtaking privilege of being a Christian? You have been given new birth. You are kept by God's power. The greatest of all inheritances is kept for you. When you face trials, they show that your faith is authentic, so that even the most painful experiences of your life will end up rebounding in praise, glory, and honor when Jesus Christ is revealed. You have received what prophets longed for, and your experience of God's grace staggers the angels.

Realize what God has done for you in Jesus Christ, and you will identify with Peter's conclusion: "Though you have not seen him, you love him; and even though you do not see him now, you believe in him and are filled with an inexpressible and glorious joy" (verse 8).

DISCOVER...

... how to prevail in your struggle with temptation.

... the secret of overcoming fear.

... how to fill up an empty life.

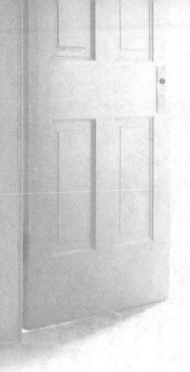

2
New Life
1 Peter 1:13–2:3

Becoming a Christian has put you in an entirely new position. A whole new life is possible now, and a new eternity awaits you when Jesus comes again. Your new birth was the beginning of your new life, and Peter is going to show us what that new life looks like in practice.

If you want a one-word description of the new life God calls us to pursue, that word would be *holiness:* "Just as he who called you is holy, so be holy in all you do; for it is written: 'Be holy, because I am holy'" (1 Peter 1:15–16).

What comes to your mind when you hear the word *holiness?* Does it seem attractive to you? People talk about a "Holy Joe," "Holy Rollers," or having a "holier-than-thou attitude." So the idea of being holy is pretty unattractive to many people.

HOLY, HOLY, HOLY

In his book *The Fight,* John White listed some of the associations that the word *holiness* first called up in his mind. They included:

Thinness	Hollow-eyed gauntness
Beards	Sandals
Long robes	Stone cells
No sex	No jokes
Hair shirts	Frequent cold baths
Fasting	Hours of prayer
Wild rocky deserts	Getting up at 4 a.m.
Clean fingernails	Stained glass

Self-humiliation

It should be a great relief for you to know that holiness in the Bible has nothing to do with any of these things.

The root meaning of the word *holy* is to cut, sever, or separate. Imagine yourself at work in your kitchen chopping celery. The telephone rings and your attention is distracted. You bring down the chopping knife and you sever your thumb.

Under these unfortunate circumstances, you could hold up the severed thumb and say, "This thumb is holy." Of course, a more useful thing would be to rush to the emergency unit at the hospital, but you get my point.

If you said, "This thumb is holy," you would mean that it is severed; it is disconnected from the body; it stands alone and is not bound up with anything else. That is the core meaning of the word *holy* in the Bible.

So when God says that He is holy, He is telling us that He stands alone. He is not bound up with anything else. He is the Creator, and He is not to be confused with the creation. He is not a product of the Judeo-Christian culture. He is who He is: separate, set apart, distinct, wholly other.

This holy God calls you to a new and different life that clearly reflects the character of the Holy One. Pursuing this life, you will often find yourself out of step with prevailing values of the culture because you are marching to the beat of a different drum.

Beginning the new life involves breaking from old ways and bonding to a new lifestyle. There are old sins to leave behind. There are new priorities to embrace. Peter shows us what this looks like when it is worked out in the realities of everyday life.

EXERCISE SELF-CONTROL

Therefore, prepare your minds for action; be self-controlled. (VERSE 13)

A good rule of Bible study is that whenever you see the word *therefore*, look and see what it's there for! *Therefore* is obviously a connecting word, telling us that what is coming is a direct consequence of what has gone before.

What has just been said here is that you have been born again. The power of the risen Lord Jesus Christ has touched your life. Now, Peter says, in the light of this reality, you need to prepare your mind for action.

Action! Holiness isn't something that happens to you. It is something that you actively pursue. Your first strategy in this battle with sin is to exercise self-control.

Now, it's one thing to say this; it's another thing to do it. Temptation is powerful. The power of habit is very strong. We hear a great deal today about addictions, patterns of ingrained response that become compulsive over time. So when Peter says "be self-controlled," some people will feel that he is being too simplistic.

The power of temptation is much stronger than any commitment that you can make. So if being a Christian was primarily about making a commitment to Jesus, then gaining control over deeply ingrained patterns of compulsive behavior would clearly be impossible.

But your becoming a Christian was much more than an act of personal commitment. You have been born again. The life of God is in you. The power of the risen Lord Jesus Christ has touched you. This puts you in an entirely new position in which it *is* possible for you to live the new life.

This is why the "therefore" that we noticed earlier is so important. The new life is made possible by the new birth. Victory over ingrained habits is possible for you because the resurrection power of Jesus has touched your life. If you think that Peter is psychologically naive, you might be underestimating the power of the Holy Spirit.

When I have the opportunity to encourage a Christian who is struggling with the power of a particular temptation, I often ask this question: Do you believe that the Holy Spirit lives in you?

Clarity about God's presence in your life is the first step to victory over the power of temptation. Your ability to exercise self-control arises from the power of the Holy Spirit in your life. Your capacity for living the new life arises directly from the miracle of your new birth.

Take a moment to get this clearly in focus: If you are a Christian believer, you have power. The Holy Spirit lives in you. The life of the risen Lord Jesus Christ has come to you. God has put you in a position where you can say no to sin. You *can* do this.

As a Christian, you have living hope of getting out of sin's grip because the risen power of Jesus is at work in you. You have living hope of getting free from pornography through the power of the risen Christ. You have living hope of overcoming the power of alcohol by this same power. You have living hope of gaining control of your tongue and temper because the power of the risen Lord Jesus Christ lives in you.

God has put you in a position where you can say no to sin. So prepare your mind for action. Victory begins in the mind, and it is planned in advance.

Sometime soon you will face circumstances that will be a temptation to you. It could be on a visit to a shopping mall where you see something you cannot afford. You experience a strong impulse to buy it on credit and add to your debt. Or it could be that you are surfing on the Internet and are confronted with an ad that invites you to a seductive Web site. Prepare your mind for action: Be self-controlled.

Your Enemy will tell you that you can't do this. Don't listen to him. You can, by the power of Christ in you.

BECOME A NONCONFORMIST

As obedient children, do not conform to the evil desires you had when you lived in ignorance. (VERSE 14)

Peter's second strategy for victory in your struggle with temptation is to become a nonconformist.

One of the most disturbing experiences for new Christians is to discover that evil desires continue to arise within you even after the new birth. In the joy of finding new life in Christ, it is natural for a new Christian to feel that sin could never be attractive again. Unfortunately, this is simply not the case.

I love the story of a new Christian who was baptized. The pastor pushed him under the water and then brought him up again. The young Christian was full of joy. Embracing the pastor, he said, "Now I won't be tempted anymore." The pastor seemed strangely subdued. "I'm afraid that for you to enjoy that blessing," he said, "I would have to keep you under for longer."

The Bible speaks to the reality of our lives, and that includes the lifelong struggle that every Christian experiences with temptation. Evil desires will arise within you. Be prepared for that to happen. And when it does, be a nonconformist.

Peter reinforces this same teaching later when he urges us to "abstain from sinful desires, which war against your soul" (2:11). I find it profoundly helpful to know that there is a war going on inside every Christian. That helps me to make sense of my own experience.

Don't be surprised or alarmed when you are tempted. That's normal. Evil desires may arise within you. Don't conform to them. Don't accept their invitation. Remember that every time you say yes to an evil desire, you increase its power over you; and every time you say no to an evil desire, you weaken its power in your life.

For example, if you have become used to buying on impulse, you will find that the urge to reach for your credit card and buy what you cannot afford is very strong. But God has put you in a position where you have the power to say no.

Don't conform to that desire! In the old life, your desires controlled you. They pushed you around. But now God has put you in a position where you are able to exercise control over your desires. Sin shall no longer be your master. That's freedom!

The Bible's teaching on sin can be summed up in three words: *Don't do it!* Evil desires will arise within you. When it happens, don't conform to them.

Don't muddy the waters by saying that you can't help it. You may have failed to do this, but that is no reason for saying that it cannot be done. The new birth has put you in a position in which you are able to fight. You don't need to conform to evil desires. And even if you have failed many times, God wants you to know that you can prevail over them.

THROW OUT THE RUBBISH

Therefore, rid yourselves of all malice and all deceit, hypocrisy, envy, and slander of every kind. (2:1)

For the last two years, our staff has observed what we call "office clear-out day." We set aside a full day to clear out files and cupboards and get rid of everything we don't need. It's a day of great joy. Music plays in the hallways as we fill our sacks with trash and make our way to the Dumpster.

The reason for all this activity is that we have a job to do, and we know that in order to do it well, we have to get rid of the clutter that would other-wise hold us back.

That's the picture here. Peter is urging us to get rid of all the clutter that would keep us from a life that reflects the holiness of God. And he gives us specific examples of the things he has in mind. Malice, deceit, hypocrisy, envy, and slander will weigh you down. So get rid of these things. Don't give them any space in your life.

Notice that God always speaks to Christian believers as those who have power. "Be self-controlled." "Do not conform to the evil desires." "Rid yourselves of all malice." Don't wait for God to do these things. He calls you to do them. And you have the ability to do them because God's power is at work in you. So get ready to take action against sin wherever you see it rearing its ugly head in your life. This will be a struggle, but God has put you in a position to fight and win. Just do it!

KEEP YOUR EYES ON THE PRIZE

Set your hope fully on the grace to be given you when Jesus Christ is revealed. (1:13)

If you ever have the opportunity of appearing on television, you will proba-bly spend some time in the greenroom, where folks who are about to appear on a program get themselves ready and wait to be invited into the studio. The whole of your life in this world is like being in the greenroom. You are here only until the moment when you will be called into the stu-dio of God's immediate presence.

Once you have grasped this, you will have a completely different perspec-tive on your life in this world. Secular society thinks that we have life now and that whatever exists after we die is only an unknown shadow. But the Christian knows that what we have now is only a shadow and that after we die, we will enter into life.

Your new life is lived between the backdrop of God's grace and the hori-zon of Christ's presence. So look at the difficulties you are facing in the light of eternity. Place the cost of following Christ in the context of the day when He will be revealed. Weigh your choices not just in the light of the difficulties now but in the light of the outcomes then. You will find that the horizon of hope will strengthen you in the pursuit of holiness.

Soon your short journey through this world will be over. Then you will stand before your Father in heaven, and you will see the face of "the Son of God, who loved [you] and gave himself for [you]" (Galatians 2:20). Learn to live every day in the light of that awesome reality. That's what Peter means when he writes, "Live your lives as strangers here in reverent fear" (1:17).

As you do this, you will be delivered from every other kind of fear. The film *Gods and Generals* tells the story of Robert E. Lee and Stonewall Jackson in the American Civil War. Jackson was given the name "Stonewall" because of his extraordinary courage on the field of battle. In one scene, after a particularly ferocious battle, one of Jackson's men asks, "General, how is it that you can keep so serene with a storm of shells and bullets raining about your head?"

Jackson replies, "My religious belief teaches me to feel as safe in battle as in bed. God has fixed the time for my death. I do not concern myself with that, but always to be ready whenever it may overtake me. That is the way all men should live. Then all men would be equally brave."

LIVE LIFE TO THE FULL

Having directed attention to the ultimate outcome of the Christian life, Peter translates convictions about the future into practical counsel for today.

> *Since you call on a Father who judges each man's work impartially, live your lives as strangers here in reverent fear. For you know that it was not with perishable things such as silver or gold that you were redeemed from the empty way of life handed down to you from your forefathers, but with the precious blood of Christ, a lamb without blemish or defect.* (VERSES 17–19)

The way of life that Peter's readers knew before coming to Christ was empty. The same was true of their forefathers. The great question that reverberates through generations and across cultures is "How do you fill up an empty life?"

Peter makes it clear that you cannot fill an empty life with silver and gold. There is nothing that you can buy or own that would redeem you from the emptiness of life. Some people try to fill up their lives with a glittering career; others with leisure, sports, travel, movies, and entertainment. But none of these things can give release from the emptiness of life without Christ. This is why it is possible to have a dream job, a great marriage, successful kids—and a growing sense of emptiness inside.

Nothing in this world can bring you the fullness of life that God wants you to know. You were created by God and for God, and your life cannot be full without Him. Careers, sports, and travel are among the many pleasures that we may pursue in this life, but they will all pass away. They are simply not big enough to be worthy of the full devotion of a human life. They need to find their place within a higher purpose.

Release from the emptiness of life is found through the blood of Jesus by which we are bought back into a new relationship with God, which begins now and will last for eternity. That is what you were made for.

Everything good in this world is a gift from the hand of God. Nothing in this world is an end in itself. Marriage is a partnership for the glory of God. Children are to be raised for the glory of God. Eating and drinking are to be done to the glory of God. Work is to be offered for the glory of God. These are the spheres in which God calls us to live for His glory. Knowing Christ lifts everything to a new level and invests every part of life with a new meaning and significance.

LEARN TO LOVE THE FAMILY

Now that you have purified yourselves by obeying the truth so that you have sincere love for your brothers, love one another deeply,

*from the heart. For you have been born again, not of perishable seed,
but of imperishable, through the living and enduring word of God.
(VERSES 22–23)*

One of the first evidences of new life is that you discover an affinity with
others who have also been born again into the family of God.

Holiness is a community project. You cannot be holy on a desert island,
because love is the heart of holiness.

The relationships that you have with your brothers and sisters in Christ are
of special importance because they will last for eternity. Christians are
born of imperishable seed. The life we share will never end.

The family of God is an outpost of eternity where holiness has begun. The
world cannot see God, but it can see Christians loving each other. So Peter
calls us to "love one another deeply, from the heart."

That's why we need to be intentional about getting rid of malice, deceit,
hypocrisy, envy, and slander (2:1). These are the things that spoil *relationships* in the family of God. You and I are going to spend eternity with our
brothers and sisters in Christ. So let's work hard at learning to love each
other now.

NOURISH THE NEW LIFE

*Like newborn babies, crave pure spiritual milk, so that by it you may
grow up in your salvation, now that you have tasted that the Lord is
good. (2:2–3)*

Your new life will be nourished by the milk of God's Word. Anyone who
has tried to comfort a hungry baby will know the intensity of a young
child's desire for milk. And anyone who has watched a small child develop
will know how quickly a well-nourished child will grow.

Your spiritual life will follow the same pattern. You have been born again,
and your new birth is the beginning of a whole new life in which God calls
you to pursue holiness. That means engaging in the fight against sin, liv-

ing in the light of eternity, and learning to love one another. God has made this life possible for you by the power of His Holy Spirit. It is your responsibility to make sure that this life is nourished as you feed on the Word of God.

DISCOVER. . .

. . . a mission worth the full devotion of your life.

. . . the supreme glory of Jesus Christ.

. . . your place in God's purpose.

3
New Purpose
1 Peter 2:4–12

Some time ago, I had the privilege of visiting several churches in northeast England. Most were quite small, and many of the people were discouraged. But one church stood out as different from the others. The members weren't a very large group, and they were meeting in a difficult area of a large city; but as we worshiped together, there was a sense of God's presence.

After the service, I asked one of the elders what might have contributed to the spiritual health of the congregation.

He described the social needs of the community—unemployment, dysfunctional families, and so forth—and explained that for many years, the services in the church had reflected the jaded discouragement of the area. The elders had met together to reflect on what might be done and had agreed that every Saturday night, each of them would pray specifically for a sense of expectancy among the believers who would gather the following day.

It was obvious to me that God had heard and answered their prayers. These believers were a light in the darkness of their community.

Many people would like to experience the light and hope of God's presence, but they don't know where to find Him. Peter wants us to know that God's presence is found among His people as we worship, live, and serve together.

Human beings face two fundamental problems: We are alienated from God and separated from each other. God's plan of salvation addresses both of these issues. He reconciles us to Himself through the Cross, and He reconciles us to each other in the church.

In our highly individualistic society, many people are intensely interested in their personal salvation and the cultivation of their own spiritual lives. They find it easy to grasp the relevance of Jesus but find it much more difficult to see the relevance of the church. For some, the problem is made worse by the obvious fact that while everything about Jesus is attractive to a Christian, the same cannot be said of the church.

Every community of believers has its failures. There are no perfect Christians, and it follows that there are no perfect churches either. So it is easy to get the idea that the church must be somewhere on the fringes of God's plan. Nothing could be further from the truth.

Now that you have experienced the new birth and begun the new life, you are ready to catch a biblical vision of God's purpose for the church and discover the joy of playing your part in the worship and witness of the body of Christ.

FINDING THE PRESENCE OF GOD

As you come to him, the living Stone—rejected by men but chosen by God and precious to him—you also, like living stones, are being built into a spiritual house. (1 PETER 2:4–5)

The simple words "as you come to him" take us to the heart of authentic worship. The "you" here is plural, like the southern "y'all"; so Peter is not talking about an individual believer praying at home. He wants us to know what happens when a community of believers draws near to God in worship.

Christian worship involves everything that we offer to Christ. This includes what we normally associate with worship—singing, praying, reading the Scriptures, preaching, and the Lord's Supper—but it extends far beyond those activities.

The church that I serve in Arlington Heights is a hive of activity—not just on Sunday mornings but throughout the week. People offer worship by making coffee, teaching Sunday school, visiting the sick, running sound systems, welcoming visitors, preparing lunch for folks who are homeless, and a host of other things. The whole life of the church is an offering of worship to God.

God is at work in all of these things. He is like a master builder who takes a pile of stones and makes them into a house. We are the stones—living stones—and as God brings us together in ministry, He is building a home for Himself.

This picture of a house where God would be at home is drawn from the temple in the Old Testament. People from all over Israel would make long pilgrimages to visit the temple because God had promised to meet them there.

The Jerusalem temple was still standing when Peter wrote this letter around the year A.D. 64. But Jesus had spoken about a day when the temple would be destroyed. This prophecy was fulfilled in the year 70, and the Jerusalem temple has never been rebuilt.

The destruction of the temple must have raised profound questions, especially for Jewish believers. They had always associated God's presence with the great building in Jerusalem. Without the temple, where on earth could God's presence be known?

Peter gives us the answer: God's presence is known wherever a community of believers gathers together to worship Jesus. In the past, God's presence was experienced among the stones of the temple. Today, God's presence is found among believers who gather to worship and serve Jesus. Worshiping communities of believers are living temples, and God makes Himself at home among them.

Having experienced the new birth and begun the new life, this is where you belong. So find a church where God's name is honored and the Bible is taught, and identify yourself with that community of believers.

People in your town desperately need a place where they can find the presence of God. That is what the church is. Jesus has promised that He will be present when His people gather in His name. The local church is at the center of God's purpose in the world, and when you grasp that purpose, you will want to be part of it.

TURNING SPECTATORS
INTO PARTICIPANTS

A holy priesthood, offering spiritual sacrifices acceptable to God through Jesus Christ. (VERSE 5)

Peter now changes the picture and uses another analogy from the Old Testament to explain how God's purpose will be fulfilled through the church. The community of believers is like a spiritual house in which God's presence is known, but believers are also priests who offer spiritual sacrifices to God.

You may never have thought of yourself as a priest before, but as a believer in Jesus, that is exactly what you are. Priests in the Old Testament were the only ones who could enter the inner courts of the temple. They were a very exclusive group drawn from the male descendants of the line of Aaron.

The normal assumption in our culture is that anybody can approach God in any way and at any time. But the Old Testament teaches us exactly the opposite. Ordinary people couldn't walk into the inner courts of the temple any more than you or I could walk into the Oval Office of the White House today.

Worship in the Old Testament was largely a spectator event. The priests had all the action. They burned the incense and offered the sacrifices. The role of the people was simply to watch.

Before the coming of Jesus, access to God had not been opened. The priests in the Old Testament were merely illustrating what would happen when Jesus came. God had promised that one day all of His people would share the privilege of serving as priests.

Today, every believer enjoys direct access to God. God's Spirit lives in you and enables you to worship and serve Christ. Worship is a "hands-on" experience for every believer.

When you first become a Christian, worship may seem to be something that other people are doing. There is a choir or a praise team. There are musicians and a pastor. There are hymns and prayers, a Bible reading, and a sermon.

Don't be a spectator. Enter into worship and it will become one of the most important areas of your spiritual growth. When you gather with other believers for worship, try to use the words of hymns and prayers as a vehicle to express your love for Christ. Let the Scriptures stretch your mind to think great thoughts about God. Allow the lines of a simple song to warm your heart to the riches of His love for you.

God is always at work when His people are engaged in worship, taking observers and making them participants. As you discover more of what He is doing, you will find that you want to sing. As you become more sensitive to the needs of the world, you will want to pray and to give. As you take the risk of getting involved in ministry, you will discover gifts and abilities you never knew you had.

When you were born again, you became one of God's priests. You have direct access to God. You don't have to ask a religious professional to pray for you. As a priest, you can pray for yourself and for others. More than that, God has put you in a position where you are able to offer spiritual sacrifices to Him. Spiritual sacrifices include anything that is offered as service and worship to God in the name of Jesus: Praise, gratitude, giving, singing, hospitality, acts of kindness, and deeds of mercy can all be offered to Him as worship, and He will take great delight in them.

THE CENTERPIECE OF GOD'S PLAN

To you who believe, this stone is precious. But to those who do not believe, "The stone the builders rejected has become the capstone," and, "A stone that causes men to stumble and a rock that makes them fall." (VERSES 7–8)

Did you know that the name "Peter" means a rock or stone? Perhaps that is one reason why Peter has so much to say about stones in this letter. He describes the Lord Jesus as "the living Stone—rejected by men but chosen by God" (verse 4) and then gives us a marvelous picture taken from the building site.

Imagine a building site where stones of various shapes and sizes are lying around. The builders arrive. They gather up some stones and bring them to the foreman, who starts sorting them out. "We can use these," he says as his skilled eye picks out the best materials.

Then he picks up a large and rather strangely shaped piece of rock. "There is no place for this," he says. "It's useless." He takes the rock and rolls it down the hill, until it comes to rest on the driveway below.

A few minutes later, a young boy comes up the street delivering newspapers on his bike. He's not looking where he is going, and the next thing he knows, the front wheel of his bike slams into the rock, throwing him over the handlebars onto the driveway.

The foreman comes down to see if the boy is all right. He helps the boy to his feet and then shouts to one of the builders, "Get that lump of rock out of here—it's nothing but trouble." So the builder picks up the rock and throws it in the Dumpster.

Later that week the mason arrives. There is an arch at the entrance to the house, and he has come to lay the capstone on the brick pillars.

"Where's my stone?" asks the mason.

"There are stones all around here," says the foreman. "Use whatever you need."

"No, I mean *the* stone, the one that was specially cut for the arch. There isn't any other like it. I sent it here to the site. Now where is it?"

The foreman realizes the mason wants the large, strangely shaped rock he had tossed, and he is embarrassed. Slowly he begins to explain that he kicked it down the hill and then threw it in the Dumpster.

The mason is furious. He runs down the hill, climbs into the Dumpster, and begins to dig in the rubble with his bare hands.

Eventually, he finds the stone he had chosen and sent to the building site. He lifts it up and holds it high above his head. "This is *the* stone," he says. Then he places the stone over the entrance to the house, where it will be seen and admired by everyone.

Jesus is the stone that the builders rejected. He came into the world, and we found no use for Him. He did not fit what this world was looking for, so we consigned Him to the Dumpster, nailing Him to a cross.

But Jesus is the centerpiece of God's plan for the human race. He is both the cornerstone on which God's building rests and the capstone that crowns all His work. God has reached into the Dumpster and exalted Him to the highest place by raising Him from the dead. "The stone the builders rejected has become the capstone" (verse 7).

STUMBLING OVER JESUS

Many have stumbled over Jesus. Peter describes Christ as "a stone that causes men to stumble and a rock that makes them fall." And then Peter explains: "They stumble because they disobey the message—which is also what they were destined for" (verse 8).

Two thousand years after His death and resurrection, many people still stumble over Jesus. They don't like His claims, and He doesn't fit what they are looking for.

Notice where the responsibility for this lies: The people who stumble over Christ are the ones who "disobey the message." It is important to remember this when we read that this is "what they were destined for." This clearly does not mean that some unbelieving people live without the opportunity of being saved. Peter makes it clear that they have exercised their choice in deciding to disobey.

A disobedient person cannot come to faith in Jesus. Repentance and faith are two sides of the same coin. The one cannot exist without the other. Faith is not possible without obedience, and obedience is not possible without faith.

Coming up against Jesus reveals who you are. When He intercepts a person's life, a decision has to be made. Some embrace Him; others resist Him, but nobody is ever the same.

DECLARING HIS PRAISE

You are a chosen people, a royal priesthood, a holy nation, a people belonging to God, that you may declare the praises of him who called you out of darkness into his wonderful light. Once you were not a people, but now you are the people of God; once you had not received mercy, but now you have received mercy. (VERSES 9–10)

In God's mercy, you have embraced Jesus. You have turned to Him in faith and begun to walk in the path of obedience. You have put your trust in Him and made Him the cornerstone of your life.

In a world that sees little value in Jesus, your calling, along with the calling of all your fellow believers, is to declare His praise. This task—this grand purpose—cannot be delegated. Believers are the only people who can do on earth what the angels do in heaven.

Our shared experience of God's grace is the glue that binds the church together. Each of us has received God's mercy through Jesus. Believers meet on level ground at the Cross and find there a common interest in declaring His praise.

Churches may not always live up to all that is involved in this, just as Christians do not always live up to all that is involved in a life of holiness, but wherever believers are gathered in the name of Jesus, these things are begun.

IMPACTING THE WORLD

Live such good lives among the pagans that, though they accuse you of doing wrong, they may see your good deeds and glorify God on the day he visits us. (VERSE 12)

Peter uses the term "pagans" to describe unbelieving people with a generally hostile attitude toward Christ and Christian believers. It would be easy and perhaps natural to feel that deeply resistant people are beyond any hope of salvation. But Peter is not ready to write off even the most hardened pagan. He has a vision of highly resistant people coming to glorify God.

Think about someone you know who may be deeply resistant to the good news of Jesus. It's hard to imagine this person coming to faith in Christ and even harder to imagine him or her praising Christ in the company of other believers. But God has called us to reach highly resistant people.

Worship and witness are the twin callings of the church, and God promises His presence as we pursue these purposes.

When Peter talks about the day that the Lord "visits us," it seems that he has in mind the day when Jesus Christ will come again in power and glory. On that day, some who were once among the world's most resistant people will join in glorifying the God who brought them out of darkness and into His marvelous light.

God is gathering people from every nation on the face of the earth. He is bringing them to faith in His Son, Jesus Christ, empowering them by His Holy Spirit, and drawing them together into purposeful communities where His praise is declared and His presence is known.

It's worth pausing to ponder this vision. Think about the folks you know who are far from faith in Christ. Now think about some of the communities and cultures around the world that are deeply resistant to His claims. Imagine the joy of being in the presence of Jesus and seeing those who were once His enemies praising Him for His grace that has saved them and transformed their lives.

It's a marvelous vision, but how will highly resistant people ever come to glorify God? The astonishing answer is "Through the good lives of Christian believers."

Our objective is to live in such a way that highly resistant people will come to glorify God. This theme takes us to the heart of Peter's letter and to the heart of the mission and purpose of the church. We're going to discover how this can work out in practice.

REACHING RESISTANT PEOPLE

Peter sets out three strategies for reaching resistant people. The first of these is to act redemptively in situations of division and conflict. God has given you the priceless gift of freedom in Christ. You can use that freedom to make choices that will bring help and healing into broken situations. God may use your acts of kindness and mercy to open the minds and hearts of people who resist the good news of Jesus.

Your second strategy will be to pray effectively. Only God can change the heart of a highly resistant person, and if we are to have any hope of that happening, we need to be in a position to exercise a ministry of prayer. That means, as we will see, guarding the relationships that God has given to us. Learning to live in such a way that nothing hinders your prayers will be critical to the impact of your life and ministry.

Acting redemptively and praying effectively may open the door of opportunity to share the good news of Jesus, but if the person you are trying to reach is to come to faith in Christ, he or she needs to hear the good news of Jesus explained in words. So your third strategy will be to speak about Jesus with the confidence that when you do, Christ will use your words and speak through you.

That's the ground that lies ahead of us in Peter's letter. We're going to learn how to pursue this great objective of living in such a way that highly resistant people will come to glorify God. That's our calling, and I can't imagine a higher privilege or conceive of a more compelling purpose.

DISCOVER. . .

. . . what it means to be free.

. . . how to respond to abuse and injustice.

. . . the power of acting redemptively.

4

New Freedom
1 Peter 2:13–25

Vachan was born in a small village in north India. He fled from an abusive home and, in the goodness of God, was taken in by a Christian family who led him to faith in Christ.

There was no church in Vachan's home village, so he gathered a small team of colleagues and began to preach the gospel there. Resistance to the team was strong. The villagers shouted warnings and threats. Then one day a crowd gathered with stones and drove Vachan and his team out of the village.

The last time I visited Vachan, he was sick. I sat at the side of his bed and was deeply moved as he told me that he had received a visit from the leader of his home village who had personally apologized for the way he had been treated. He then asked if Vachan would begin a Christian ministry in the village and offered land that could be used for building a Christian hospital.

By any standards, this was a remarkable change of attitude in a community that had shown itself highly resistant to the gospel. Vachan had no doubt as to how this change happened. Christian believers had continued to show love, kindness, and mercy toward the village people, and their works had opened a door for their words.

God has given us the challenge of living in such a way that highly resistant people will come to glorify Him. In a world that is increasingly hostile to the good news of Jesus, that means learning how to act and speak in ways that open a path for people to come to Christ. That's how God calls us to use our new freedom in Christ.

UNDERSTANDING THE AUDIENCE

Live as free men, but do not use your freedom as a cover-up for evil.
(1 PETER 2:16)

Peter's cry of freedom in verse 16 would play well with any American audience, but the fascinating thing about this statement is that his first readers didn't have any of the freedoms that we enjoy. They were living under the iron fist of the Roman Empire, and Rome was becoming increasingly intolerant toward Christian believers. Just two years after Peter wrote this letter, the infamous emperor Nero launched a violent persecution against Christians. He covered believers in pitch and burned them as living torches in his garden parties. And yet Peter tells these believers to live as free men!

As well as being oppressed by the state, Peter's first readers suffered injustice and exploitation at work. Some of them were slaves (verse 18), and there doesn't seem to be much freedom in that! It's important to say that the Bible gives no support whatsoever to slavery. But it does give wise and practical counsel to believers who suffer injustice and exploitation and have no hope of getting out.

The Bible speaks to the world as it is, not as we would like it to be. It is not a blueprint for an ideal world that only exists in our imagination. It is

God's Word for this fallen world with all its pain and suffering. Those who are oppressed and exploited will find help for dealing with the realities of life here.

Then, in addition to the burdens of political oppression and economic exploitation, some of Peter's first readers were struggling with serious difficulties at home.

It seems that in the early church a number of women had come to faith in Christ, but their husbands did not share the same commitment. This meant that the women lived with a spiritual mismatch in this most intimate area of their lives.

So Peter's readers were oppressed by the state, exploited at work, and unhappy at home. And Peter tells them to "live as free men"! But what kind of freedom can you enjoy if you are persecuted, exploited, and fundamentally unhappy?

Peter wants you to know about a freedom you can experience even in the most unhappy circumstances. Grasping this freedom may be one of the most liberating experiences of your life.

WHAT IS FREEDOM?

Freedom is the ability to make a different choice.

I have a friend who says that he was brought up in a family where everything was forbidden except for what was compulsory. There's not much freedom there either. Freedom means that you have the ability and opportunity to do something different.

Let's think through what this would mean in practice for Peter's first readers. Given that they were oppressed by the state, you would expect them to live in perpetual conflict. Since they were exploited at work, you would expect them to be filled with hatred. If they were facing great difficulties at home, you would expect them to cut their losses and leave.

But freedom means that you have the ability to make a different choice.

Freedom means that you don't have to hate your employer if he or she treats you badly. You don't have to leave your spouse if you are unhappy. You don't have to become enmeshed in conflict with a school or business if they have acted inappropriately. You are free! You have the ability to make a different choice!

Without Jesus, we don't have nearly as much freedom as we like to think. Jesus made this clear when He said, "I tell you the truth, everyone who sins is a slave to sin" (John 8:34). Sin is like a strong current in a river that carries us in one direction. You may think that you are free as you swim with the current, but that is an illusion. You're not really free unless you have the ability to go against the current.

This is the priceless gift that Jesus gives to every believer. When you came to Him, He set you free and gave you the ability to choose.

Nobody has ever enjoyed greater power and freedom than Jesus. People who have great power normally use that power to make their own lives more comfortable. But Jesus models a different way.

All of His choices were geared to reconciliation. And these choices, made in the face of the most intense hatred and conflict, are an example for us to follow. These liberating choices include the freedom to display integrity and to withhold retaliation.

CHOOSING INTEGRITY

"He committed no sin, and no deceit was found in his mouth."
(VERSE 22)

I have met many people who struggle to find faith because of the sin of a Christian believer that has affected them deeply. Integrity is our first priority in seeking to win others for Christ.

The integrity of Jesus was in His words as well as His actions. There was no deceit in His mouth. Truth is often the first casualty of conflict.

There are times when telling the truth can get you into serious trouble. When you get into a situation like that, the pressure to use lies and deception to save your own skin can seem almost overwhelming. But Jesus used His freedom to make a different choice. In an atmosphere of intense antagonism and hostility, Jesus was brought before Caiaphas, the high priest, who asked Him if He was the Son of God.

For those who watched, the tension of the moment must have been unbearable. But Jesus answered plainly, "It is as you say. . . . But I say to all of you: In the future you will see the Son of Man sitting at the right hand of the Mighty One and coming on the clouds of heaven" (Matthew 26:64). On hearing this, the high priest tore his robes, and the council of seventy leaders spat on Jesus and struck Him with their fists.

Then Jesus was sent to Pilate. Pilate asked Him if He was the king of the Jews. Again Jesus replied plainly. "My kingdom is not of this world . . . [though] you are right in saying I am a king" (John 18:36–37). After that, Pilate had Him scourged.

Most of us will never face a situation where the physical cost of speaking the truth will be anything like what it was in the experience of Jesus. But there are many ways in which we face the same pressure to twist words to suit an audience.

In a marketing culture, churches experience increasing pressure to reshape and repackage the gospel to fit with what people want to hear. Jesus never chose this road. He spoke and acted with integrity even when that meant losing followers who were offended by His words.

Obviously we must use Christian wisdom and good judgment in choosing what to say to unbelieving people and when to say it, but Peter is reminding us that we do not have the option of reshaping the gospel. If we are serious about seeing change in highly resistant people, our first responsibility is integrity in our actions and our words. That involves being faithful to the truth even when that truth is not popular.

Choosing Not to Retaliate

When they hurled their insults at him, he did not retaliate. (VERSE 23)

If you have ever been in a situation where you have been humiliated, robbed of your dignity, and made to look foolish, you will know that the desire for revenge can seem almost overwhelming. Think about the humiliation Jesus experienced. They dressed Him in a scarlet robe, placed a reed in His hand, and pressed a crown of thorns on His head. Then they spat on Him. They took the stick and hit Him over the head again and again.

Think of the retaliation that Jesus could have made at that moment. He only had to speak the word, and the angel armies of heaven would have turned Calvary into a wasteland of scorched earth. But Jesus made a different choice. He did not retaliate.

Perhaps there is a situation in your life where you have been wounded and would love to get even. God may give you that opportunity, and then you will face a choice. If your aim is to defeat your enemy, retaliation may be a good option, but if your aim is to win him or her over, you will want to consider a different path.

The desire for revenge is natural when you are wounded. But freedom means that you do not have to go down that road. Christ has put you in the position where you can make another choice.

Refusing to Make Threats

When he suffered, he made no threats. (VERSE 23)

If someone hurts you, you will instinctively want to hit back hard. If you can't do that now, you may find yourself thinking about how that might be done in the future. That's where threats begin.

Think about the threats Jesus could have made to His enemies. He is the Son of God. He will decide the eternal destiny of every person who has ever lived. He could have threatened Caiaphas and Pilate with hellfire and damnation. But He made a different choice.

Threats involve the nursing of a grievance. They put you in the position of carrying an unhealed wound into the future. They close off the possibility of reconciliation by locking you into resolution based on revenge.

Throughout the agonies of His suffering, Jesus remained focused on His mission. He came into the world to seek and save lost people, and the way He responded to His enemies is an example for us. If we want to win over highly resistant people, we must choose integrity and avoid retaliating or making threats.

TRUSTING THE JUDGMENT OF GOD

He entrusted himself to him who judges justly. (VERSE 23)

From the example of Jesus, Peter now shows what we should pursue. Jesus did not regard the abuse that He suffered as something that should be swept under the carpet and forgotten as if it had never happened. Jesus pursued justice. Yet He did not pursue it through retaliation but by trusting the ultimate justice of God the Father.

God is just. The reason that you have a sense of and desire for justice is that God has placed that within your heart. And you can be absolutely certain that there will be justice for every evil that has ever been committed. God has set a day on which He will judge the world in righteousness; on that day, He will bring every dark secret to light.

This is something for which we should be profoundly thankful. If we could not count on God to bring justice on the Last Day, we would be under tremendous pressure to deal with every injustice now.

It is a huge relief to know that there is One who judges justly. You can choose to entrust to Him injustices that have been perpetrated against you and wounds that have been inflicted on you. In doing so, you will be following the example of Jesus.

Jesus trusted the world's most terrible injustice and its most awful abuse into the hands of God, and when He did that, He knew that one of two things would happen. Either those who perpetrated this awful deed would be brought to complete justice in the presence of God, or they would cast themselves on the mercy of God and find forgiveness through what He suffered. And since Jesus' mission was that highly resistant people would come to glorify God, the latter would bring Him the greatest joy.

CHOOSING TO ACT REDEMPTIVELY

He himself bore our sins in his body on the tree, so that we might die to sins and live for righteousness. (VERSE 24)

This is one of the most profound and wonderful statements in the whole Bible. When Jesus died on the cross, our sins were laid on Him. There is an obvious uniqueness about this. Only Christ could bear the sins of the world. But Peter's emphasis in these verses is on how Christ's death is an example and a pattern for us.

If someone wounds you and you choose to retaliate, you reflect the pain that you have experienced back onto them. But if you choose not to retaliate, you will find that you absorb the pain into yourself. The pain ends with you because you choose not to pass it on. This is what Jesus did. He chose to act redemptively. Christians are the only people in the world who can follow His example.

FOLLOWING THE MASTER'S EXAMPLE

Christ suffered for you, leaving you an example, that you should follow in his steps. (VERSE 21)

The suffering of Jesus was a sacrifice for us to trust, but it was also an example for us to follow. Now let's try to apply this practically. Suppose that you are in a situation where you have been deeply wounded by someone who is obviously in the grip of great darkness. What should you do?

On the one hand, you are committed to justice and you are drawn to pursue it. On the other hand, you have compassion and you wonder if you should let the matter go.

This calls for great wisdom, and there are no easy answers. But if you are committed to following the example of Jesus, you will want to begin by asking how you can act redemptively. What course of action is most likely to bring healing?

Sometimes the best hope of redemption for a person lies through confrontation. This is often the case with people who are engaged in patterns of self-destructive behavior. The best hope of God's grace breaking into their darkness is often through love that cares enough to confront. That's what happened when the prophet Nathan went to King David and exposed his secret sin of adultery. That was precisely what David needed. Nathan's aim in the confrontation was to win David at a time when he had become highly resistant to God's truth.

There are situations in which it is right to bring a matter for justice in a court of law. There are situations in which it is right for a church to exercise discipline. But there are other situations in which you may choose to absorb the pain and to forgive because "love covers over a multitude of sins" (1 Peter 4:8).

The question that will guide your decision is always the same. What course of action is going to bring the best chance of seeing God's grace break through in the life of a person who is in great darkness?

Freedom means that you have a choice. Ecclesiastes 3 reminds us that there is a time to embrace and a time to refrain. There is a time to tear and a time to mend. There is a time to speak and there is a time to be silent. There is a time to fight and there is a time to refrain from fighting. The way you discern the time is by remembering the objective.

The Bible does not offer guaranteed outcomes for any choices that we make, but if we are serious about seeing people who are deeply resistant to the good news of Jesus Christ coming to glorify God, then let's use our freedom to make some different choices.

Are you willing to use your freedom to act redemptively? Cultivate the habit of applying this principle to every situation of conflict you face. Choose words and actions that, as best you can tell, are most likely to bring healing. And remember that acting redemptively is more important than being heard or winning an argument.

We will not change our places of work by endless conflict. We will not heal our marriages by insisting on our way. We will not change the world by insisting on our rights.

In a world that is consumed with conflict, God has given us the freedom to make a different choice that reflects the character and example of Jesus. The impact of your life will depend in large measure on the way you use that freedom.

DISCOVER. . .

. . . why God sometimes tunes out our prayers.

. . . wisdom for winning unconverted family members.

. . . . the secrets of lasting love and beauty.

5

New Relationships
1 Peter 3:1–12

What do you think might be the world's all-time most embarrassing situation for a Christian believer? Let me suggest one good contender, found in the Old Testament story about a famous prophet.

Jonah was God's man in his generation. When he spoke, people listened, and lives were changed through his ministry.

Then God called him to work in a new location. Change is never easy, and Jonah didn't want to go. So he found a ship and sailed in the opposite direction. It was a flagrant act of disobedience to God.

Sometime into the journey, the ship was caught in a great storm. The crew began to panic. None of them knew anything about the God of the Bible, and in the middle of this crisis they were looking for help. In utter desperation the captain of the ship asked Jonah to pray.

What a moment! Jonah was surrounded by an entire crew of pagan sailors, and these highly resistant people were asking for prayer!

But Jonah couldn't do it. He had to admit that he couldn't pray because he was running from God. No doubt that qualifies as one of the world's most embarrassing situations.

No Christian wants to be useless, especially to an unbeliever who is desperate. God has given you the objective of living in such a way that highly resistant people may come to glorify Him. If you want to fulfill that purpose, you have to be in a position where you are able to pray.

Your prayers can be hindered. And hindered prayers can block your relationships with God and others.

PRESSING THE MUTE BUTTON

Some people are convinced that God will hear any prayer offered by any person in any way and at any time, but the Bible makes it clear that this is simply not the case.

Effective praying flows from right living. It is the prayer of a *righteous* person that is "powerful and effective" (James 5:16). This teaching runs all through the Bible. The person who can stand in God's holy presence is the one who has "clean hands and a pure heart" (Psalm 24:4).

This is why we can only pray effectively through the Lord Jesus Christ. The name of Jesus is not a tagline added by Christians to round off their prayers. It is a fundamental recognition that our hope of being heard by almighty God rests entirely on our being cleansed through the blood of Jesus.

Obviously we cannot pray in the name of Jesus while consciously holding on to something that we know to be wrong. King David said, "If I had cherished sin in my heart, the Lord would not have listened" (Psalm 66:18). David was not suggesting that a person has to be perfect before God will hear his or her prayer. God listens to the prayers of a sinner, but He does not listen to the prayers of those who are intent on holding on to their sin.

Jesus applied this same teaching by making it clear that there would be no point in a person coming to worship while turning a blind eye to an unresolved conflict. "If you are offering your gift at the altar," He said, "and there remember that your brother has something against you, leave your gift there in front of the altar. First go and be reconciled to your brother; then come and offer your gift" (Matthew 5:23–24). The way you treat other people affects your relationship with God.

I often get frustrated with the advertisements on television, so I've developed the habit of pressing the mute button when they come on and doing something else until the program I'm watching resumes.

In a sense, when God sees me acting in a way that is unkind toward the people He has placed next to me, He presses the mute button on my prayers. That means that it would be possible to spend an hour in prayer, or even go on a day retreat and achieve absolutely nothing of lasting spiritual value.

One of our greatest dangers in the Christian life is a false spirituality that separates our relationship with God from our relationships with other people. It's easy to get the idea that spirituality is about personal prayer, small group Bible study, or Sunday worship. These are all good things, but none of them will be of any value if God has pressed the mute button on our prayers.

MARRIAGE MATTERS

God has a purpose for your new life. Your objective is to live in such a way that highly resistant people will come to glorify God. Your first strategy is to speak redemptively. Your second is to pray effectively. So you need to make sure that nothing hinders your prayers.

Keeping the channel of prayer open is the central theme in this section of Peter's letter. Christian husbands are to treat their wives with respect "so that nothing will hinder [their] prayers" (1 Peter 3:7). Believers are to seek peace and pursue it because "the eyes of the Lord are on the righteous and his ears are attentive to their prayer" (verse 12).

If we are to fulfill our God-given purpose, we need to be able to pray effectively. For those who are married, this involves nurturing their husbands or wives. And for all Christian believers, it means developing healthy relationships within the family of God.

Of course, you don't have to be married in order to be useful to God. Peter was married, but Paul was single, and God used him to spread the gospel across the Roman Empire.

Nor do you have to be happily married. Some of the people who have been most remarkably used by God have endured terrible marriages. John Wesley would be one example. His marriage was a disaster from the beginning, and it never improved, but God used him to bring revival to a whole nation in the eighteenth century.

Becoming a Christian may not transform your marriage, but it will change you. Your calling is not to have a perfect marriage or family, but to honor God in the unique setting of your home. Peter gives us a picture of what that looks like for wives and for husbands.

FOR WOMEN ONLY

Wives, in the same way be submissive to your husbands. (VERSE 1)

There is hardly a more controversial passage of Scripture in our culture than this one, and so it is especially important to make sure that we understand what God is saying.

The first question any Christian wife would reasonably have is what this submission might look like in practice. Peter explains the kind of submission he has in mind by giving an example. He points us to the examples of "the holy women of the past who put their hope in God" and says, "They were submissive to their own husbands, like Sarah, who obeyed Abraham and called him her master" (verses 5–6).

I find it significant that God should identify Sarah as the model for

Christian wives. Sarah was no pushover. She was a strong-willed woman, and she knew how and when to draw a line.

There must have been times when Sarah's life was almost impossible. She had made her share of mistakes, just as Abraham had made his. One of them was her suggestion that Abraham should have a child by her servant Hagar. It was a suggestion born of desperation. God had promised that Abraham and Sarah would have a child, but since Sarah was already old, she found the idea laughable (Genesis 18:10–12). Conceiving a child through Hagar seemed much more practical, and that's how Abraham's first son Ishmael was born.

Then God stepped in and fulfilled His promise. Sarah conceived in her old age and gave birth to Isaac. After Isaac was born, Sarah decided the time had come for Hagar and Ishmael to make their own lives elsewhere. Abraham didn't like that idea at all. But Sarah was right. We know that because God told Abraham to do what she said (Genesis 21:12).

Women who follow the example of Sarah will not give unthinking, slavish obedience to their husbands. God does not call you to be a cheerleader when your husband is headed in the wrong direction. There are times when your husband may need you to say, "I think this is wrong." Sarah did that. She was as the voice of God to her husband, and there may be times when God calls you to that ministry too.

The important thing was that Sarah looked up to Abraham and treated him with great respect: She called him "master." The word Peter uses here was a term of respect meaning "Sir" or "Mr." This sounds exceedingly strange to us today, but it is telling us that Sarah did not look down on Abraham. She did not roll her eyes and make him out to be foolish. She held him in the highest respect and played a wonderful role in making him the great man of God he became.

God calls you to follow Sarah's example in your marriage. Nobody can play a greater role in enabling your husband to become the man God calls him to be than you. Following Sarah's example, you will experience the blessing of God and fulfill His purpose.

Think of how God's purpose for the world was advanced through this remarkable woman. It was Sarah who gave birth to Isaac, and it was through this line of descent that Jesus Christ was born into the world.

Sarah could never have imagined what God would do through her love and loyalty to Abraham, but this lady's faithfulness to her husband will result in a vast crowd of once highly resistant people from every tribe and nation glorifying God for all eternity.

WINNING A CAPTIVE AUDIENCE

So that, if any of them do not believe the word, they may be won over without words by the behavior of their wives, when they see the purity and reverence of your lives. (VERSES 1–2)

Peter is speaking to all wives, but he draws particular attention to the difficult situation of a Christian wife whose husband does not believe. Both partners face unique pressures in this situation. If your husband does not believe, he will not be able to understand your love for Christ. He may accept your faith and support you in it, but your new life is a mystery to him.

On your side, there will be an intense desire that your husband will come to share your faith in Jesus. This is natural, but the intensity of your longing carries its own dangers. Peter makes it clear that the most effective strategy for winning an unbelieving husband is not through your words but by your behavior.

Bible expositor Warren Wiersbe tells the story of a woman who desperately wanted to see her husband come to faith in Christ. So she turned on the radio and kept religious programs playing loudly through the house. Her aim was that her unsaved husband would hear the truth. "All she accomplished," Wiersbe says, "was to make it easier for her husband to leave home and spend his evening with his friends."

That rather extreme example illustrates a powerful principle for all of us who are anxious to win a close relative to faith in Christ. The unique hazards of trying to win someone within your immediate family circle come from the fact that within the family you have a captive audience. That's what makes the situation so pressurized, both for you and for the other person.

Maybe you have a son, daughter, brother, sister, father, or mother who does not know the Lord. If that's your situation, Peter has some practical wisdom for you. Don't abuse the privilege of a captive audience. Pull back on the words. Use them very sparingly. Over time, the quality of your life will speak far louder than your words.

THE SECRET OF LASTING BEAUTY

Your beauty should not come from outward adornment, such as braided hair and the wearing of gold jewelry and fine clothes. Instead, it should be that of your inner self, the unfading beauty of a gentle and quiet spirit. (VERSES 3–4)

Peter is not placing an apostolic ban on fancy hairstyles, jewelry, or designer-label clothes. He is not saying you can't wear them. He is saying your beauty should not depend on them.

Far from being a legalistic restraint, this Scripture is absolutely liberating. We live in a culture where there is tremendous pressure on how you look. Now let's face it: Not many of us look in the mirror and say, "Wow!" Most of us look in the mirror and say, "Oh dear!"

How you dress and how you keep your hair is important. It will attract the attention of your husband. But the unfading beauty of a gentle and quiet spirit will attract the attention of God, and God will use this to make a deep impression on your husband too.

In Old Testament times, the temple was overlaid with gold to make it a beautiful place for the presence of God. But now you are God's temple. The Holy Spirit lives in you, and your life will be made beautiful for God's presence not by the gold you may wear but by the unfading beauty of your gentle and quiet spirit.

Some women have told me that they have problems with this verse. I can understand why. At first sight it might seem as if Peter is calling wives to a soft-spoken quietness that would be unnatural for a woman whose style is vivacious, determined, or forceful. It's helpful to remember that nobody was ever more forceful than Jesus, and yet He was gentle. His strength was under control. He was the point person for the greatest mission in the history of humanity, and yet in the intensity of His life and ministry, He enjoyed an inner peace and stillness.

Gentleness and strength belong together. A sparkling personality and the peace of a quiet spirit are natural partners. A gentle and quiet spirit attracts attention *to* Jesus because it is a reflection *of* Jesus.

So cultivate the kind of beauty that can't be bought in a store. The poise, grace, and beauty of your inner life is of great worth in God's sight, and it will never fade away.

For Men Only

Husbands, in the same way be considerate as you live with your wives. (VERSE 7)

If you're a husband, knowing and understanding your wife is your greatest privilege and your biggest challenge. Literally translated, Peter's call to husbands is to live with your wife "according to knowledge."

Your wife is not like any other woman God has ever made. Your job is to know her and to understand her. Learn what makes her happy and pursue it. Discover what hurts her and avoid it.

Your wife has unique struggles, fears, hopes, and dreams. You need to understand them and then let that knowledge shape the way you relate to her.

God has called you to listen to her with your heart. Never let it be said that her friend or her counselor understands her better than you do. Work at getting to know her until it can truly be said that you understand her better than anyone else.

Remember that this is your lifelong calling. Your wife is not the woman you dated five, ten, twenty, or thirty years ago. Discover who she is today. Understand what God is doing in her life now, and live with her according to knowledge. Living out this one statement will change you and your marriage.

STRENGTH AND HONOR

Husbands . . . treat [your wives] with respect as the weaker partner and as heirs with you of the gracious gift of life, so that nothing will hinder your prayers. (VERSE 7)

Treating your wife with respect means honoring her by placing her in a high and exalted position. Your wife has chosen to give herself to you. A large part of her happiness or misery will flow from the way that you treat her. So make sure that you regard her as a sacred trust from God.

Cherish your wife. Honor her with your time and your money. Use your strength to support her and to bless her. Speak *to* her in a way that makes her feel that she is honored. Speak *about* her with praise, so that she will be exalted in the eyes of others.

Peter describes your wife as the weaker partner, a description you might not recognize if you are married to a forceful woman. There is a growing trend in Western society for women to become the front-runners in family life, and one effect of this is that husbands can become lazy when it comes to marriage and the family.

Men who know how to take initiative and make things happen at work can sometimes be surprisingly passive at home. Don't fall into that trap. God wants you to be an initiative-taker in the interests of your wife and family.

The importance of these things is clear from the reason Peter gives for pursuing them: "so that nothing will hinder your prayers." If you want to be useful to God, make sure that you do everything possible to cultivate your marriage. Changing the world begins at home. Living a life of love starts with loving those God has placed next to you.

SOMETHING FOR EVERYONE

What Peter says to husbands and wives in the home sets the track for all believers in the wider circle of our relationships in the body of Christ.

> *Finally, all of you, live in harmony with one another; be sympathetic, love as brothers, be compassionate and humble. . . . For the eyes of the Lord are on the righteous and his ears are attentive to their prayer. (VERSES 8, 12)*

These are words that we can pass over quickly. They seem predictable and perhaps even a trifle dull, but they really matter. God's blessing rests on His family when our relationships are in good repair (see verse 9). God's people will see good days when we "seek peace and pursue it" (verse 11. And the ultimate reason for choosing this often difficult path is that God hears our prayer as we pursue it.

A friend of mine was chairing a church meeting that got rather ugly. I don't know what the issue was, but people were divided, and they did not do a good job of expressing their differences kindly.

Tempers became frayed and words were spoken in anger. The pastor was not able to guide the meeting to agreement, and eventually, somewhat defeated, he turned to his assistant and asked him to close the meeting in prayer.

The assistant pastor politely but firmly declined. I'm not sure how helpful that was, but I understand why he didn't feel at liberty to pray. God's family had been squabbling, and as long as the squabbling remained un-resolved, there was no point in pretending that God would listen to their prayers.

Cultivating healthy relationships in the home and in the church is critical to fulfilling our mission in the world. Our primary strategies in reaching out to highly resistant people are to act redemptively and to pray effec-tively. Our top priority is to live in such a way that nothing hinders our prayers.

Learn to place the tensions, arguments, and disputes that arise in your home and in your church in the larger setting of your life's purpose and your usefulness to God. When you see how much your relationships matter, you will discover a new motivation to reflect the character of Jesus where it matters most.

DISCOVER. . .

. . . why a word can be worth a thousand pictures.

. . . how Jesus experienced hell on the cross.

. . . how Christ can speak to others through you.

6

New Confidence
1 Peter 3:13–22

The debate between John F. Kennedy and Richard Nixon in the 1960 presidential election was a turning point for communication in America. Polls showed that a majority of those who heard the debate on the radio thought that Nixon had won, while a majority of those who saw the encounter on television thought the debate belonged to Kennedy.

The reason for this discrepancy was simple. Kennedy looked great on TV. Clean-shaven and dressed in a sharp dark suit, he looked presidential, and his image added credibility to his words. In contrast, Nixon looked unimpressive. His eyes shifted, his face seemed gray, and TV viewers were distracted by what they saw.

God has called us to penetrate our culture with the good news of Jesus Christ, and that means communicating verbally *and* visually. Highly resistant people need to see God's grace in action before they are ready to hear it explained in words. That is why our first strategies in reaching others must be to act redemptively and to pray effectively. But demonstrating the gospel in action will not be enough to bring a person to faith in Christ. The message must be put into words.

WORDS AND PICTURES

God speaks to us in words and pictures. He speaks visually in the creation and verbally in the Scriptures. I love to travel in the mountains. Their breathtaking beauty tells me that God is great. But I cannot tell from the mountains that God loves me. I can look at the moon and the stars and perceive something of God's power. But the moon and the stars cannot tell me that God sent His Son to die for me or that Christ rose from the dead on the third day or that He is coming back in glory to judge the living and the dead.

For this we need words, and that is why God speaks to us verbally in the Scriptures. The Bible is like a pair of spectacles, bringing the fuzzy picture that we have of God in the creation more clearly into focus.

Words and pictures are both powerful means of communication. Pictures have the power of impact. Words have the power of content. When Gutenberg invented the printing press, a whole culture was formed around the power of written words. But we live in the age of video, and our culture is increasingly formed around the power of images. So it is important that we do not forget the significance of words.

One communications expert demonstrated the power of words by asking his students to communicate the following simple statements in pictures:

1. The cat sat on the mat.
2. The cat is not on the mat.
3. The cat was on the mat.
4. The cat likes to be on the mat.
5. The cat should not be on the mat.
6. Get off the mat, cat!
7. If the cat doesn't get off the mat I shall kick it.[1]

I reckon that I could make a reasonable attempt at communicating the first two statements in a picture, but I would struggle with the third, and I would be in serious difficulty with the rest.

Some things can only be communicated in words. I could draw a picture to communicate the fact that Jesus died on the cross, but if I wanted to communicate that He died on the cross for my sins, or that the one dying on the cross was the Son of God, or that the Son of God who died on the cross calls me to repent, I would have to use words.

Highly resistant people are often like hard ground that needs to be opened up before a seed can be planted. Acting redemptively and praying effectively may bring a person to the point where they are ready to receive God's truth, but if they are to come to saving faith in Christ, somebody has to put the good news of Jesus into words.

READY TO ANSWER

Always be prepared to give an answer to everyone who asks you to give the reason for the hope that you have. (1 PETER 3:15)

If someone you know has a new brightness in their eyes or a spring in their step, you might guess that they have fallen in love or that they have come into some big money. Your curiosity is aroused, and you start guessing at what the reason might be.

The same thing will happen when unbelieving people look at you. Your new birth has brought you into a living hope through the resurrection of Jesus, and there is something irresistibly attractive about genuine hope.

A normal Christian life will provoke questions, and when they arise, you need to be ready to give an answer. God has spoken to us visually and verbally through the creation and the Scriptures. Our calling is to mirror that pattern of communication so that His truth can be seen in the new creation of our lives and heard in the testimony of our words.

Giving a *reason* for your hope will help another person to see how they can discover the hope that you enjoy. If what has happened to you is simply an experience, then it is unique to you and of little value to anyone else. But if there is a *reason* behind your experience, the same hope is open to others also.

Your hope arises directly from your faith in the risen Lord Jesus Christ (1 Peter 1:3), and for this reason the same hope is open to others who put their trust in Him. You may not be gifted as a speaker, but you can explain to another person that Jesus is the reason for your new life and your living hope.

God will use your words and speak through them. That's the main point of the next section of Peter's letter. Frankly, it's one of the most difficult passages in the New Testament, but with a little patience and thought, you will grasp its main point, and I think you will be encouraged at how directly it applies to your life.

DID JESUS GO ON A JOURNEY TO HELL?

Christ died for sins once for all, the righteous for the unrighteous, to bring you to God. He was put to death in the body but made alive by the Spirit, through whom also he went and preached to the spirits in prison who disobeyed long ago when God waited patiently in the days of Noah. (VERSES 18–20)

Pause for a moment to take in this magnificent statement of the good news. Jesus, the perfectly righteous Son of God, died for you, and when He did this, He accomplished everything necessary to bring you to God.

The difficulties begin with the next statement, where Peter tells us about Jesus preaching to spirits in prison who disobeyed God in the time of Noah. Some people think this means that after Jesus died and before He rose again, He went down into hell and preached the gospel to people who had died in Old Testament times.

If that were true, it would mean that these people had the opportunity of repenting, believing, and being saved after they died. Indeed, a growing number of teachers claim that people may have the opportunity to decide for Christ after death and that some people in hell may finally be translated into heaven.

It's easy to see why this passage in 1 Peter comes up in this discussion. If Jesus preached the gospel in hell, why should we not believe that even in hell, there will be the opportunity for people to be saved?

If it were the case that those who do not receive Christ in this life will have another opportunity later on, I would feel that we should recall most of the missionaries sent out from our church. Some of them are putting their lives on the line in the Middle East, Africa, and Indonesia. They have undertaken the hardest task in the world, and frankly, if highly resistant people will have the opportunity to find life in Christ after death, it really isn't worth it.

The idea that Jesus went on a disembodied journey to hell between His death and resurrection to preach the gospel to people who had died centuries before raises several difficulties.

First, Peter never says that Jesus descended into hell. Look carefully and you will see that there is no reference to hell anywhere in this passage.

Second, why did He preach only to the spirits who disobeyed in the time of Noah? Why would He not preach to those who disobeyed in Sodom and Gomorrah or anybody else who disobeyed for that matter?

Third, the idea that some people might be given a second chance to repent after death goes against the plain teaching of Scripture. It is appointed for each person to die, and after that comes the judgment (Hebrews 9:27).[2]

WHEN HELL CAME TO CALVARY

Those who believe that Jesus preached in hell between His death and resurrection often quote from the Apostles' Creed, a great historic statement of the Christian faith, which says about Jesus: "He suffered under Pontius Pilate, was crucified, dead and buried. He descended into hell."

Jesus did enter hell, but not through a visit there between His death and resurrection. Hell came to Calvary on the day Jesus died. He experienced all the dimensions of hell on the cross.

The crucifixion of Jesus lasted for six agonizing hours. The trial and scourging of Jesus took place early in the day, and He was crucified at nine o'clock in the morning. Many things happened during the next three hours. The crowd taunted Him. Religious leaders mocked His claims. Thieves who were crucified beside Him hurled abuse.

Then, at midday, God stepped in. Darkness covered the whole land. This was not an eclipse. Jesus was crucified at Passover when there was a full moon, and besides, an eclipse does not last for three hours. The darkness at Calvary could only be explained by a direct intervention of God.

Jesus was now entering the heart of His Passion. It began as He suffered at the hands of His friends: Judas betrayed Him, Peter denied Him, and the rest forsook Him and fled. It intensified as He suffered at the hands of His enemies: He was scourged, mocked, condemned, and nailed to the cross. But at midday, Jesus began to experience another dimension of suffering at the hand of God, and when this happened, God turned off the light.

Jesus' suffering during these three awful hours of darkness is indescribable. Peter has already told us that Jesus "bore our sins in his body on the tree" (2:24). That is what was happening in the darkness. He carried the weight of the accumulated guilt and shame of the world. The wrath of God was poured out on Him. He was cut off from the comfort and love of God the Father. And throughout this suffering He was in a conscious agony of body and soul. That is hell, and Jesus tasted every dimension of its pain on the cross.

Jesus' descent into hell was not a disembodied visit for preaching between His death and resurrection. It was the heart of His suffering as He bore the penalty of your sin on the cross. He entered hell so that you should never know what it is like. Take a moment to pause and worship.

PREACHING THROUGH NOAH

He was put to death in the body but made alive by the Spirit, through whom also he went and preached to the spirits in prison who disobeyed long ago when God waited patiently in the days of Noah while the ark was being built. (VERSES 18–20)

Now we're ready to discover how Jesus preached to the disobedient folks in the time of Noah, and to find out what all this has to do with you and me today.

Peter wants us to know that the same Jesus who died and rose again spoke by the Holy Spirit through Noah. When Noah spoke, Jesus was speaking through Him.

Those who heard Noah were highly resistant to his message. They continued in their disobedience to God, and that is why their spirits are in prison today. But Christ spoke to them during their lifetime through Noah.

Now, here's the encouragement for you: When Noah spoke God's truth, God spoke through him, and when you speak about Jesus, Jesus speaks through you.

The Lord Jesus Christ speaks in every age by His Spirit through His people. When you have an opportunity to explain that Jesus is the reason for the hope that is in you, the Holy Spirit will take your words and use what you say as a means of Jesus speaking to that person.

This will help you to gain confidence in speaking about Jesus. God speaks to people who do not know Him through ordinary Christian believers who are ready to explain that their hope is found in Jesus.

DON'T GET DISCOURAGED BY SMALL RESULTS

God waited patiently in the days of Noah while the ark was being built. In it only a few people, eight in all, were saved through water. (VERSE 20)

Of all the characters in human history, God chose Noah as the model for our ministry. That is significant. Noah's generation was the most wicked in all of human history. Corruption and violence had multiplied, and God sent the Flood on them because He saw that the thoughts of that generation were "only evil all the time" (Genesis 6:5).

If you have found that some of the people around you are hard to reach with the gospel, then spare a thought for Noah. God called him to speak to the most resistant people who have ever lived (2 Peter 2:5).

Noah didn't see great results from his preaching. In fact, at the end of his entire life of ministry, only eight people were saved. That should teach us to be cautious about how we measure results.

The important thing about Noah's ministry was that Christ spoke through him. This did not mean that vast crowds of people repented and believed. But they did hear the voice of Jesus.

Ministry among highly resistant people isn't easy. What matters is not the number of people you lead to Christ, but your faithfulness to Christ in the place where He has set you. And if He has set you in a tough place, don't get discouraged by small results.

YOUR SIGNIFICANCE
IN GOD'S PURPOSE

There are only two occasions in the history of the world when a judgment from God will fall on the whole world. The first judgment was in the time of Noah. The last judgment will come when Jesus returns in power and glory to wind up human history as we know it.

The task of declaring God's truth before the first judgment was given to Noah. The task of declaring God's truth before the final judgment is given to us.

God has put you in Noah's shoes. He has given you the wonderful privilege of speaking to others in His name and on His behalf. Your ministry matters. Your words about Jesus to a friend, colleague, or neighbor may be the means that the Holy Spirit uses to bring them to faith in Christ and change their eternal destiny. So don't ever underestimate your significance in God's purpose.

God will be at work when you choose to act redemptively, pray effectively, and speak courageously. This is how highly resistant people who do not know Him and desperately need to hear from Him will come to know the truth.

SAILING TO A NEW WORLD

In it [the ark] only a few people, eight in all, were saved through water, and this water symbolizes baptism that now saves you also. . . . It saves you by the resurrection of Jesus Christ, who has gone into heaven and is at God's right hand—with angels, authorities and powers in submission to him. (VERSES 20–22)

Noah's ark is a wonderful picture of Jesus Christ. God told Noah to enter the ark. It must have taken an act of faith for him to do this: The ark was on dry ground, and there was no sign of rain in the sky! But Noah believed God's promise and acted on it. He gathered his family and got into the ark. Then God closed the door, and the judgment He had spoken about began.

Rain fell from the heavens, and springs of water rose from the earth. The ark rose, carrying Noah and his family safely through the judgment and into a new world.

When you take the step of believing God's promise and putting your trust in Jesus, the Bible describes you as being "in Christ." Just as Noah was brought safely through the first judgment in the ark, so Christ will bring all who are in Him safely through God's final judgment on the world.

Being "in Christ" saves you and that's why Peter speaks here about baptism. Peter is not suggesting that being baptized saves you in itself. Baptism is the sign of a person identifying fully with Jesus, and it is being "in Christ" that saves you because He has risen and "has gone into heaven and is at God's right hand—with angels, authorities and powers in submission to him" (verse 22).

Noah didn't have an easy life. God called him to a tough ministry. He was not privileged to lead a great revival in which hundreds turned to God in repentance and faith. But Christ spoke to the people of Noah's generation through him. God was faithful to His promise and brought Noah safely through the Flood and into a whole new life. This same God will be faithful to you throughout your life, and then He will bring you safely through the judgment into eternity. That gives you solid ground for living with confidence.

CONFIDENT, NOT FEARFUL

Do not fear what they fear; do not be frightened. (VERSE 14)

Let's review what we have learned: You can be confident in sharing the reason for your hope with others because when you speak about Jesus, Jesus speaks through you. And you can live with confidence because the Christ who died for you will never let you go.

Having grasped these things, we are in a better position to see why Peter calls us to live above the level of fear. In the early days of the church, many people were afraid of the power of the state. The Roman Empire was a brutal tyranny, and one of the ways in which the early Christians demonstrated the presence of Jesus in their lives was by living with confidence when others were living in fear.

I'm convinced that the specter of fear is one of our greatest challenges—and opportunities—today. The rise of terrorism, the spread of cancer, and the uncertainty of the national economy have all contributed to a climate of fear. As a Christian believer, you have a unique opportunity to show that knowing Jesus makes it possible to live with confidence in an uncertain world.

Such confidence in a fearful world will make even highly resistant people stop and listen.

NOTES

1. James Montgomery Boice and Eric J. Alexander, *Whatever Happened to the Power of Grace?* (Wheaton, Ill.: Crossway, 2001), 52.

2. I am indebted to Larry Dixon for his insight into these verses in his book *The Other Side of the Good News* (Tain, Scotland: Christian Focus, 2003).

DISCOVER...

. . . how to make a decisive break with sin.

. . . why your obedience matters today.

. . . how to identify your spiritual gifts.

7

New Urgency
1 Peter 4:1–11

One of the challenges of being a parent comes when your kids ask questions to which you don't know the answer. Thankfully, you don't have to be able to answer every question in order to be a good parent. And that isn't a requirement for being a good Christian either.

I say that because we are about to encounter a bump in the road. Our aim has been to learn the Christian life from 1 Peter, and our commitment has been to follow the teaching of this letter wherever it leads. That has meant taking each paragraph seriously, discovering what it says, seeing how it relates to what has gone before, and applying its teaching to our own lives today.

I hope that by the end of this study, you will feel that this is something you can do for yourself. God has given the Holy Spirit to every believer. He opens your eyes to the truth, and with His help, you can understand the Scriptures.

The Bible belongs to ordinary Christians. God has spoken to *us,* and He has done so in language that we can understand. But from time to time, you will come across verses in the Bible that are hard to understand. I think that happens twice in 1 Peter. We've just passed the first example when we read about Christ preaching to the spirits in prison through Noah. It's certainly not obvious what that means. Now we come to the second example, where Peter says, "He who has suffered in his body is done with sin" (1 Peter 4:1). What on earth does that mean?

As you study the Bible, you will come across some things that are hard to understand. You might be encouraged to learn that even the apostle Peter felt that when he read Paul's letters (2 Peter 3:16)! So don't worry when you come across something that isn't immediately obvious to you.

Some of the world's greatest minds have wrestled to understand the Word of God over thousands of years. If you have a question about the Bible, you can be pretty sure that somebody else has asked it before. So don't panic. Ask someone who knows more than you do or check out a Bible commentary; if you still can't find an answer, file the question away in a "to be answered later" folder that you can keep on paper or in your mind. Thankfully it's possible to see the big picture even when you don't have all of the pieces.

THE PRICE YOU
PAY FOR DOING RIGHT

Therefore, since Christ suffered in his body, arm yourselves also with the same attitude, because he who has suffered in his body is done with sin. (1 PETER 4:1)

When you come across a difficult Bible verse, it is usually helpful to see how it fits with the rest of the passage. The Bible is the Word of God, and God has spoken in a way that is coherent.

Peter has been talking about the way in which Christians may suffer for doing what is right (3:14, 17). So the kind of suffering that he has in view is not the misfortune of a broken leg or the trial of needing surgery. It is specifically the price that you pay for doing what is right.

Many believers look back to the time they said a prayer, went forward at a meeting, or were baptized as the moment when their new life began. But you will not be walking with Christ for long before He brings you to a crossroads where it becomes obvious that following Him will cost you something.

This will be a defining moment in your Christian life. When you pay a price for doing what is right, and make a decision you would never have made if it were not for Jesus, you have some skin in the game, and there will be a new clarity in your obedience.

I recently spoke with a believer from Eastern Europe who had experienced the pressure of living as a Christian under communist rule. When I asked him about how his church had changed since the fall of communism, he told me that it has doubled its size and halved its strength. He was far from convinced that greater freedom had been a blessing to the church.

Faith that has a low cost usually has a low value. So you should not be surprised if God puts you in a situation where following Jesus will involve a sacrifice for you. And when you pay the price, you will find your determination to make a decisive break with sin is strengthened.

Time Is Running Out

He who has suffered in his body is done with sin. As a result, he does not live the rest of his earthly life for evil human desires, but rather for the will of God. (VERSES 1–2)

The time for making a decisive break with sin is now! Peter longs for every Christian believer to come to this point quickly so that we can get on with the work that God has given us to do. Once you have understood your calling in this world, it will be obvious that you don't have the time to go on messing about with sin. Living for evil human desires is a thing of the past. Your future is about fulfilling the will of God.

Peter presses home the urgency of this in three ways. First, God will give you a limited amount of time to fulfill His purpose in this world. Your time is running out.

Second, the unbelieving people around you have a limited amount of time before they are called into the presence of God. Their time is running out.

Third, God has set a day when He will intercept the time line of human history. Jesus Christ will return in power and glory and gather all believers into His presence. That day is drawing near. Then the whole church will be gone. So our time is running out.

YOUR TIME

For you have spent enough time in the past doing what pagans choose to do. (VERSE 3)

Many of Peter's first readers could look back to years lived without Christ. These years had been wasted in drunkenness, carousing, and the like. Peter did not remind them of this to build regret, but to press home the urgency of living wholeheartedly for Christ now.

Life is moving on. Your years are slipping by. Soon you will stand in the presence of Jesus to give an account of your life. That time draws nearer every day. You simply haven't got time to carry on compromising with sin.

None of us knows how long we have to live, but I find it helpful to think of a normal life span in stages. There are your years in school, your years of building a career or raising a family, your years of midlife, and your years of retirement; and you only get one run at each stage.

You get one chance to do the will of God at high school. One chance to be sold out for Christ at college. One run at raising a godly family, one run through the dangerous waters of midlife, and one chance to finish strong in your retirement.

There is never a convenient time for doing the will of God, and it is dangerously easy to slip into the pattern of thinking that you will live for Christ fully at the next stage of life.

A Christian who is messing about with sin is of no use in the purpose of God. In ice hockey, a player who commits a foul is sent to the penalty box. In Britain we call that the "sin bin." Players in the sin bin are out of the game. Peter says, "You have spent enough time there. God wants you back in the game."

Don't make the mistake of letting another day go by messing around with sins that you should have left behind long ago. You have a limited amount of time in which to make your life count for God.

THEIR TIME

They think it strange that you do not plunge with them into the same flood of dissipation, and they heap abuse on you. But they will have to give account to him who is ready to judge the living and the dead. (VERSES 4–5)

Christians aren't the only ones whose time is running out. The clock is ticking for those who do not believe as well.

Remember that our objective is to live in such a way that highly resistant people will come to glorify God. Highly resistant people have a limited amount of time to come to Christ. Their clock is also ticking, moving relentlessly toward the day when they will be brought to account in the presence of God.

Peter explains that this is why "the gospel was preached even to those who are now dead" (verse 6). In just thirty years after the Day of Pentecost, the good news of Jesus had spread all over the Roman Empire. Highly resistant people came to faith in Christ. Churches were planted. Missionaries were sent out. Then gradually, the first generation of believers were called home into the presence of Jesus.

When a believer dies, he or she is "judged according to men in regard to the body" (verse 6). Death is God's universal judgment on all human sin, and believers share this common experience of fallen humanity. Christians die as men die in the body, but they live as God lives in the spirit (verse 6). The triumph of the gospel is that when you die, you will live, and that is why it is so important that the good news of Jesus should be preached.

The folks you rub shoulders with are going to die, and when that happens, they are going to give account to God. They need to hear and believe the gospel so that when they die, they can live, and the urgency of this is that their time is short.

OUR TIME

The end of all things is near. (VERSE 7)

On one great day, when "the end of all things" comes, the Lord Jesus Christ will return in glory. The church has from now until that day and not a moment longer, to fulfill the work that God has given us to do. That's our time.

Nobody knows when Jesus Christ will return, but the Scriptures make it clear that this event could happen at any time. God has orchestrated a chain of strategic events through the course of human history, beginning with the creation, continuing through the Old Testament, the birth, death, and resurrection of Jesus, the gift of the Holy Spirit, and today, the ministry of the church.

The next event on God's calendar is the return of the Lord Jesus Christ in glory. When that happens, believers will be caught up to meet Him in the air. We call this the rapture of the church. What happened to Jesus at the ascension will happen to all of us together. And it will happen in a moment, "in the twinkling of an eye" (1 Corinthians 15:52).

This will not be the end of world history. The Bible speaks of other events that will continue after believers have been taken into the presence of Jesus. But it will be the end of our time. God has given us the task of bringing the good news to all people, and we don't have forever to do it.

So there are three clocks, each counting down a limited amount of time known only to God. Any one of them could go off at any time. I have the time that God gives to me, and I do not know when that will end. Unbelievers around me have the time that God gives to them, and I cannot tell when that might end for any one of them. And the church has the time that God gives until Christ returns, and that could come at any moment.

There is an urgency about bringing the gospel to lost people in our cities, suburbs, universities, businesses, and schools. There is an urgency about communicating the good news of Jesus in the Muslim world, the Hindu world, the Far East, and central Africa.

The church was born in an explosion of spiritual life and vitality on the Day of Pentecost. Persecution had caused believers to be scattered across the Roman Empire, and everywhere they went they took the gospel with them. Two thousand years later, it is easy for us to settle down into a predictable routine in which church is part of our lives organized for our convenience, and we forget why we are here. Our task is great. Our time is short. The end is near.

DISCOVER YOUR SPIRITUAL GIFT

Each one should use whatever gift he has received to serve others, faithfully administering God's grace in its various forms. (VERSE 10)

Once you have discovered the urgency of the Christian life, you will want to know how you can be most useful to the Lord. The best way to play your part in fulfilling God's purpose is to use the gifts that He has given to you. Every believer has been given some gift and ability that is useful in serving Jesus Christ.

Peter identifies speaking and serving as specific examples of these gifts. Other passages in the New Testament give different examples including encouraging, leading, acts of mercy, administration, and helping others (see Romans 12, 1 Corinthians 12, and Ephesians 4). There is some overlap in these lists of gifts, and none of them is the same. So it seems that the gifts listed in the New Testament are a sample of the kinds of things that God graciously equips His people to do.

In the Old Testament, we read about other gifts. Skilled craftsmen worked with wood, stone, and precious metals to make the ark of the covenant. Their skills were gifts from God, offered back to Him for work that was geared to the advance of His kingdom (Exodus 31:1–5). Gifts of music also come from the hand of God, as do gifts of relating to young people, skills to listen, the ability to communicate compassion, the list is endless.

One of the most delightful pictures of God's people functioning effectively comes in the book of Nehemiah, where we read about the rebuilding of the city of Jerusalem. Builders were building; teachers were teaching; leaders were leading; choirs were singing. The whole community was engaged in the great task to which God had called them. That is how God's work gets done.

New Christians often feel that they have little to contribute to ministry. You may think that many years will pass before you are able to be useful to the Lord. Nothing could be further from the truth.

God is your Creator, and He has uniquely gifted you. Your natural abilities all come from Him and can now be offered back to Him. God always makes wise use of His resources. So you can be confident that He intends to use the abilities He has already given you to serve and bring blessing to others.

More than that, since you are a believer, the Holy Spirit lives in you. He will add to your gifts as He equips you for ministry. One of the joys of your Christian life will be to discover the new gifts and abilities that God has given you for ministry and service in His kingdom.

Try to find out what God has equipped you to do. Some simple questions will help you. What do you enjoy doing? What have you done that seems to have been followed by God's blessing? What can you see that needs to be done? Different people see different needs and that in itself can be a good indicator of the kind of ministry that you can offer to the Lord.

If you are not sure about your gifting, ask another Christian who knows you well. And don't let the fear of failure hold you back. Most people who have found the ministry that God has for them got there through a process of trial and error.

MINISTRY PRIORITIES

Ministry is a great privilege, but it can often seem overwhelming. Multiple needs, inadequate resources, and limited time conspire together and can cause us to feel helpless.

Facing the challenges of such needs, Peter reminds us of the gift of prayer. "The end of all things is near. Therefore be clear minded and self controlled so that you can pray" (verse 7). Notice the connections. Nobody can pray in a panic. Effective prayer comes from a clear mind. That is why it is a good thing to use the Bible as fuel for your prayers. If you come to the Scriptures with faith, God will use His Word to settle your mind in times of pressure. Then you will be able to pray.

Peter's second ministry priority is love. "Above all, love each other deeply, because love covers over a multitude of sins" (verse 8). Knowing that time is short will give you a different perspective on grievances and arguments that can consume a great deal of time and energy. If the church is engaged in the work of ministry, there just isn't time for them.

You make different decisions when you know that time is short. A husband and wife are arguing. They say unkind words. The next day he is in a car accident and he is gone. If they had known it was their last evening, they probably would not have argued, and if they had, they would have resolved it.

There are many ways of resolving a dispute, but the quickest one is to forgive. If you are able to do that, it will enable you to get on with the ministry that God has given you.

JUST DO IT!

If anyone speaks, he should do it as one speaking the very words of God. If anyone serves, he should do it with the strength God provides, so that in all things God may be praised through Jesus Christ. To him be the glory and the power for ever and ever. Amen. (VERSE 11)

Ministry gets done as each member of the body of Christ uses their gifts to fulfill the work that God has given them to do. Time is short, so make sure that you find out how God wants you involved in ministry, and then do it with all your heart. Then we will be able to do all that God has called us to accomplish.

If you have a gift of hospitality, open your home to others gladly; do it without grumbling. If you are a speaker, make sure that you teach the Word of God. If you are serving in some other capacity, do it in the strength God provides. God will sustain you in everything He calls you to do for as long as He calls you to do it.

When a church sees that the time is short, then we will get praying, loving, and serving, and who knows how many highly resistant people will live to thank God that we did.

DISCOVER...

. . . what to do with your unanswered questions.

. . . the dangers of claiming more than God has promised.

. . . how your struggles can be your greatest encouragement.

8

New Reality

1 Peter 4:12–19

Sometime in your Christian life you will find yourself living with an unanswered "Why?" There's no avoiding this experience. It comes to us all. You throw yourself into following Christ, and then you experience something that just doesn't make sense. You find yourself asking "Why?" and there seems to be no answer.

I think about friends who long to have a child but have been unable to conceive. They love the Lord and struggle to understand why He has not answered their prayers as they hoped. Then I think about a pastor who led a missions trip to India. His church prayed for his ministry and then was shocked to hear the news that he had been involved in a car accident and died as a result of his injuries. Why?

Sooner or later you will be faced with a situation of suffering and loss where you find yourself speechless. You will wonder how to relate your faith in an all-powerful and all-loving God to the reality that you cannot avoid, and you will have no use for sentimental platitudes.

When that time comes, it will be important for you to know that you are not alone. Christians who live with an unanswered "why" stand in a long and honorable line that includes Peter's first readers, and goes all the way back to our Lord Jesus Christ. Others have walked this way before.

Manuals for new Christians don't usually include a section on pain, suffering, or unanswered questions, but 1 Peter does, and I'm grateful for that. The Bible is not like a glossy brochure advertising an idyllic Christian life while discreetly hiding the struggles in the small print. God's Word tells it like it is and helps us to shape realistic expectations for living by faith in this fallen world. And that is one of the most important keys for unlocking the Christian life.

GREAT EXPECTATIONS

Dear friends, do not be surprised at the painful trial you are suffering, as though something strange were happening to you. (1 PETER 4:12)

From the earliest days of the church, there were evidently some people who came to faith in Christ and then were taken by surprise when their lives were rocked by some unexpected trauma. Their first thought was that painful trials had no place in the life of a believer, and so they felt that their experience must be highly unusual.

Their expectations were shaped by the assumption that if we belong to a loving God, we should experience a comfortable life. Nobody expects to have a completely trouble-free life, but it is natural to feel that if God really cares for us, He will make things right with the main issues of our lives, like our families, our finances, our health, our freedom from pain, and our safety.

False expectations lead to bitter disappointment, so Peter addresses the issue of expectations directly. Painful trials in the Christian life are neither surprising nor unusual. They are normal.

UNREALISTIC EXPECTATIONS

Some Christians find this difficult to accept, so it's worth pausing to identify some unrealistic expectations that may exist in your mind or in the minds of other Christians around you. Here are five examples.

1. Christians always have happy marriages.

False. If you marry a difficult person, you can expect to have a difficult marriage. Temperaments clash in believers as much as in unbelievers. Some husbands are unloving, and some wives display the opposite of a gentle and quiet spirit. That's reality, and that is why Peter had to write about these issues. You may be ready to respond to the Scriptures with faith and obedience, but others in your family circle may not have come to that point. God may do a miracle at any time, but there is no promise in the Bible that guarantees a happy marriage to every believer.

2. Christians no longer struggle with sin, doubt, or fear.

False again. We no longer are under the power of these things, but we are not yet saved from their presence. Sin, doubt, and fear are our constant enemies. They are always attacking us and sometimes they prevail. That's why Peter urges us to confront the sinful impulse within us whenever it rears its ugly head (2:11). The reality is that we find ourselves engaged in a lifelong struggle with hypocrisy, envy, and a host of other sins. When we gain the upper hand against one temptation, it's not long before we become aware of a new struggle with another sin that we had not recognized before. The battle never ends.

3. Christians feel pain less because Christ is with them.

Definitely false. People often get confused here. The apostle Paul said that Christians do not "grieve like the rest of men, who have no hope." These words from 1 Thessalonians 4:13 are often read at a funeral service, and some Christians have mistakenly thought this means either that we shouldn't grieve, or that the grief of believers doesn't hurt as much as the grief of other people. Christians have a hope for the future that shines into our grief, but the grief of a Christian who loses a loved one is every bit as deep as the grief of one who does not believe.

Read the book of Job and let your expectations be formed from the Bible. Our hope of the resurrection tells us that there will be joy and victory beyond the pain. Until then, we have the comfort of God's presence in the pain, but these things do not make the pain less.

4. Christians should not need medication if they are trusting in Christ.

That is false. We live by faith in the Son of God, but we also live this life in the body (Galatians 2:20), and the functioning of that body is directly affected by its chemical balance. There is no difference between a believer and an unbeliever at this point. If you give Christian kids too much sugar, they will be hyperactive. The health of a Christian is affected by diet and exercise in exactly the same way as an unbeliever. An overactive or underactive thyroid will affect the energy and mood of a Christian or a Muslim in exactly the same way. A great deal of unhappiness could be avoided if believers who need medication would just take it.

5. Christians are safer, healthier, and wealthier than other people.

False. God has never promised that a Christian is less likely to have a car accident or to be the victim of crime or to suffer from cancer than any other person. Those who care for their bodies, are good stewards of their money, and take care over their safety might expect to enjoy the benefits that flow from their wisdom, but there is no reason to think that there is any significant difference among Christians, Buddhists, Hindus, or Jews in this regard. The persecution recounted among believers in 1 Peter is one indication that Christians should expect to face difficulties simply because of our association with Jesus.

When Jesus invited people to follow Him, He urged them to count the cost. People who start out with unrealistic and unbiblical expectations will not follow far. They live in a fog of confusion, frustration, and disappointment, in which they eventually lose their way. That's why grasping the reality of the Christian life is so important.

RECOGNIZE THE ROLE OF SUFFERING

Watch out for teachers who claim more than is promised in the Bible. Any teaching that does not recognize the role of suffering in the Christian life is unbiblical and unrealistic. It may sound magnificent, but it is inadequate. Teaching that does not recognize the honored place of pain in the experience of a believer is simply not big enough for life.

Some years ago, a book was published entitled *I'm OK, You're OK*. That phrase captures the false impression that Christians sometimes convey in the church: "I'm OK, you're OK. Come and join us in the fellowship of the OK, and you will be OK too."

But that's not reality. The truth is that Christians are a mass of contradictions. We love Jesus, but we struggle with the flesh. We have faith, but we struggle with many doubts. We are forgiven, but we are not yet wholly free from sin. We have discovered the truth, but there are many things that we do not understand. We experience God's comfort, and yet we feel the pain of our failures and loss.

Authentic Christian fellowship begins when we take off the rose-tinted spectacles. Then we will be able to encourage each other as we face the reality of our struggles.

Biblical expectations of the Christian life should be shaped by three realities: (1) We live in a fallen world; (2) we follow a crucified Savior; and (3) we are still in the process of being saved.

CHRISTIANS LIVE IN A FALLEN WORLD

Do not be surprised at the painful trial you are suffering, as though something strange were happening to you. (VERSE 12)

We usually refer to the sin of our first parents, Adam and Eve, and its disastrous effects as "the Fall." The first sin was the beginning of a pattern of rebellion against God that has run through history and continues today. We have been born into a fallen world that suffers all the effects of human rebellion, and painful trials are not strange in a fallen world.

Our world is on a collision course with its Creator. We are members of the human race that is at war with God. God will win this war against His enemies, but He has offered an amnesty to any who will give up the fight against Him. He invites us to surrender to Him in repentance and faith, and to all who do, He promises that He will take us out of this world before His final judgment comes. But until that day, we continue to live in the war zone. We are caught up in all the effects of a world that has chosen a path that leads to destruction.

In our culture, many children are brought up to expect the world . . . so Christian parents need to tell their children what kind of world to expect. We must tell our children about this fallen world—about the First World War where thousands died for no good reason and the Second World War where millions died because of an appalling evil. We need to tell them about the holocaust and the genocides in Cambodia and Rwanda. We need to tell them about terrorism, including September 11 and the Oklahoma bomber.

Wise parents won't want to tell all these things to their children at one time, but you will want to help them develop a Christian view of this world, created perfectly by God but tragically fallen through sin and now living under sin's awful curse.

Human pride is always dreaming of a perfect world where there will be peace, harmony, and universal happiness. But we cannot make it happen. These things await Christ's return when all things will submit to His authority. Until then, Christians share the common lot of humanity.

We don't belong to this world but we do live in it, and so we share in its experience of sickness, loss, tragedy, disaster, and death. Faith in Jesus is not a strategy for avoiding these trials. It is our strength in facing them.

CHRISTIANS FOLLOW
A CRUCIFIED SAVIOR

Rejoice that you participate in the sufferings of Christ, so that you may be overjoyed when his glory is revealed. If you are insulted because of the name of Christ, you are blessed, for the Spirit of glory and of God rests on you. (VERSES 13–14)

Christian expectations of life in this world should be shaped by the fact that we have chosen to follow a crucified Savior.

Following a glamorous celebrity may mean sharing in the glamour, but following a crucified Savior is likely to be a very different experience. Jesus spoke to His disciples about this plainly. "In this world you will have trouble," He said. "If the world hates you, keep in mind that it hated me first" (John 16:33; 15:18).

Your experience will always reflect what you are invested in. If you are in business and it is a tough time for business, then it will be a tough time for you. If you have invested in stocks or bonds, then what happens to them will happen to you. One of the most common descriptions of a Christian is that we are "in Christ," and if you are in Christ, it would be reasonable to expect that you will share in His experience. That will include what Peter describes here, "participat[ing] in the sufferings of Christ" (verse 13).

Let's take a moment to consider Jesus' experience of life in this world, and as you do, think about ways in which you might have shared His experience.

1. He worked hard in manual labor, making a living that was never more than enough to get by.
2. He was never married, and He had no children.
3. He never became a homeowner. In fact, He had no place to lay His head.
4. He was the special focus of Satan's particular attention and was tempted with greater force than any man has ever been tempted.

5. He was the most underappreciated person who ever lived; rejected in His own hometown, He was a prophet without honor in His own country.
6. He experienced the constant frustration of colleagues who did not understand what He was saying and were reluctant to follow where He was going.
7. He knew the deep pain of being betrayed by one in whom He had placed great trust.
8. When He faced His hour of greatest need, His friends let Him down.
9. When false charges were brought against Him, there was nobody who would help Him find justice.
10. He reached out to wounded people, yet experienced hatred from the very people He had chosen to love.

That's what life in this world was like for Jesus. And you have chosen to follow Him. So if your experience at any point is the same as His, that's par for the course. Learn to shape your expectations by the life and experience of Jesus.

That sounds tough, but there is, of course, a magnificent upside to living in this new reality. Those who share in Christ's sufferings will also share in His glory (verse 13). Jesus is risen and exalted at the right hand of the Father, and if you are in Christ, this will happen to you!

Peter has already explained that your trials will demonstrate the authenticity of your faith. He makes the same point here. If you are insulted, mocked, ridiculed, or persecuted for Jesus' sake, you have the clearest evidence that you belong to Christ. That's why Peter says, "You are blessed, for the Spirit of glory and of God rests [present tense] on you" (verse 14). Peter is not suggesting that a person who suffers will have a new or different experience of the Holy Spirit, but that the difficulties you face in following Jesus are in themselves evidence that you are a true follower. The pressures you experience because of the name of Christ show that God's Spirit rests on you.

This is why Peter speaks about ". . . judgment begin[ning] with the family of God" (verse 17). Obviously he does not mean judgment in the sense of condemnation. "There is now no condemnation for those who are in Christ Jesus" (Romans 8:1). The word *judgment* refers to a test that can have either a positive or a negative outcome. The judges at a race are not there to condemn the athletes, but to judge what has been achieved by each one. An athlete spends months preparing for the big race, and when that moment comes, the evidence and effect of his or her training will be seen. Try to think about your trials, frustrations, and disappointments as the great moments of your life. This is where all that God has been doing in your life will be made known.

CHRISTIANS ARE IN THE PROCESS OF BEING SAVED

It is hard for the righteous to be saved. (VERSE 18)

The Bible speaks about salvation in three tenses: It is a completed transaction, a continuing process, and a future hope. The reality is that you have been saved, you are being saved, and one day you will be saved! Let's look at these three statements more closely.

Looking back, you have been saved from sin's penalty. "It is by grace you have been saved, through faith" (Ephesians 2:8). A transaction took place when you came to faith in Jesus in which the power of His shed blood was applied to your life. Your sins were forgiven. Your judgment was taken. The deal has been done.

Looking forward, one day you will be saved from sin's presence: Peter spoke about, "The salvation that is ready to be revealed in the last time" (1:5). When Christ returns, He will take you into His presence where there will be no more death or mourning or crying or pain. Then He will make a new heaven and a new earth, which will be the home of righteousness. All the effects of the human rebellion that we experience in this fallen world will be a distant memory. Sin will hold no attraction to you. It will be outside and unable to enter your unclouded experience of the joy and beauty of God's marvelous new creation.

But sin still holds some attraction for believers now, and so until that day, we are in the process of being saved from sin's power. "To us who are being saved [present tense] it [the cross] is the power of God" (1 Corinthians 1:18). That's what Peter is talking about here when he says, "It is hard for the righteous to be saved." He doesn't mean that it is hard to put your faith in Jesus or that it will be hard for Jesus to take you into His immediate presence. But every Christian knows that the ongoing struggle with sin's power is hard, and that struggle is part of the reality of the Christian life.

If you think that the Christian way is easy, these words are a warning. It is hard for the righteous to be saved, so if you find it easy, there is good reason to question whether you are really a Christian. Followers of Jesus engage in a struggle against sin throughout their lives, and if you don't know much about that struggle, you have good reason to question whether you are really saved.

But if you are finding that the Christian way is hard, these words should come as a wonderful encouragement to you. If the Bible said that the Christian life is easy, I would be wondering what is wrong with me! But when I hear that it is hard for the righteous to be saved, it helps me to make sense of my experience.

When you came to Christ, you may have thought that your troubles were over, but now you have found that there are more struggles going on in your soul than ever before. That's the surest sign that you are on the right path.

A Christian is like a fish swimming upstream. You are going against the currents of the world, the flesh, and the devil. Any dead fish can float with the current of the river, but it takes life, strength, and energy to go against the stream.

It's not easy to overcome a sin that you've struggled with for many years. It's not easy to maintain your passion for serving Christ throughout a lifetime, and it's not easy to see others enjoying a blessing that God did not give to you. But your continuing struggle through the difficulty of all these things is the evidence that you are going in the right direction.

Don't be surprised by the painful trials of your life. You live in a fallen world, and you follow a crucified Savior. God isn't finished with you yet. You are still in the process of being saved, and that process isn't easy.

But remember that God's Spirit rests on you, and because you belong to Christ, you will one day share His glory. Don't be discouraged. Keep pressing on. Commit yourself to your faithful Creator and continue to do good (verse 19).

DISCOVER. . .

. . . hidden signs of the presence of pride.

. . . freedom from the tyranny of self.

. . . how to cultivate spiritual growth.

9

New Humility

1 Peter 5:5–7

Have you ever had the feeling that you were moving forward when actually you were standing still? It happened to me the other day when I was driving in Chicago. I had stopped at lights in heavy traffic and was looking out of the side window, when suddenly I felt myself moving forward.

I slammed my foot hard on the brake, but it made no difference. I guess it was only a split second later that I realized the car beside me was moving backward into a parking space, but for a moment I felt quite sure that I was being propelled forward to disaster.

It's easy to get the idea that you are moving forward in the Christian life when actually you are standing still. It is possible to pour yourself into serving Christ and yet to lose your usefulness, and the way that most easily happens is through the subtle but deadly snare of pride.

Your struggle with pride will continue throughout your Christian life. The power of other temptations is often tied to particular seasons of life, but pride is an enemy that will stalk you all your days. In the last chapter of his letter, Peter speaks to Christian leaders about the pressures they face (1 Peter 5:1–4) and to young men about challenges that are unique to their stage of life (verse 5). But then he identifies one issue that is a challenge for all believers: "All of you, clothe yourselves with humility toward one another, because, 'God opposes the proud but gives grace to the humble'" (5:5).

IT DOESN'T COME NATURALLY

There will never be a point in your life where it is easy or natural to be humble. Some battles become easier over time, but not this one. Pride is like flour in a mill: It gets everywhere, and more is produced every time the mill is working. You are always trying to keep it down, but you never fully clear it up. Nobody is free from this struggle.

Charles Spurgeon, a famous preacher in the nineteenth century, told of a lady who came up to him after a service and said that she prayed every day that he would be kept humble. Spurgeon thanked her, and then asked her if she was praying the same thing for herself.

"Oh no," she said, "there is no need for that. I don't think that there is any tendency in me to be proud."

That's the subtlety of pride: We are never in so much danger of being proud as when we think that we are humble. I laughed at myself recently when I received a letter from the president of our denomination asking me to speak at our annual conference on the subject of "Giving up your ego." I was grateful for the invitation and for the subject, and my first thought when I read it was, "Oh, they must think I'm humble." And of course I lost it right there!

C. S. Lewis points out that if a Christian becomes humble, one of Satan's most subtle strategies is to draw his or her attention to this fact, with the aim of making the person proud of his or her humility! Pride is like a cataract that grows over the eye so that we no longer see ourselves clearly.

THE LADDER OF HUMILITY . . . AND PRIDE

Back in the twelfth century, a monk by the name of Bernard of Clairvaux was asked by a friend to write a book on humility. He said that he didn't know enough about the subject, but that he did know from experience about how a person can fall into pride, and so he offered to write about that.

He pointed out that you take the same road to enter a town as you use to leave it, and so, if you want to learn about humility, you can do so by discovering what makes you proud, and moving in the opposite direction. Then he compared humility and pride to steps on a ladder. Pride takes you up, humility brings you down, but the steps on the ladder are the same, and they can take you in either direction. Bernard called his book *The Twelve Steps of Humility and Pride*. It has been a helpful guide to many Christians for nearly a thousand years, and it is well worth our pausing to learn from his insights.

Bernard identified curiosity as a first step to pride. The inquisitive person, he said, looks up to some people as his betters and down on others as his inferiors, and as soon as he does this, he begins to feel envious of some and scornful of others.

"One moment he soars to the heights in his pride, and the next he sinks to the depths through envy," Bernard wrote. Both are examples of pride because it is love of his own excellence that brings him distress when others surpass him and joy when he surpasses others.

He's right. You can see the pattern running throughout life. It begins in school where the seniors don't want to be caught hanging out with the freshmen. It continues in business where people form estimates of other people's importance from the amount of money they make. It can be expressed among pastors in casual conversation comparing notes on how many people are attending different churches. Whenever we measure ourselves against others, we are manifesting pride.

On one occasion after His resurrection, Jesus spoke to Peter about the future. Peter's immediate reaction was to ask what the future would hold for John. Jesus said, "What is that to you?" (John 21:22). In other words, "Mind your own business." That's a very important principle because as soon as I begin measuring myself against others, I have taken the first step to pride.

BEING FLIPPANT OR BOASTFUL

Another step identified by Bernard is flippancy. He described a man who is increasingly controlled by levity and loses the capacity to be serious. "You rarely see this person sigh or cry. If you think about it, his faults seem to be either forgotten or forgiven. . . . He is always making jokes and never misses an opportunity to laugh."[1] Pride keeps a man from looking at himself seriously. It causes him to skim through life without examining his own soul.

Flippancy can become a mask, hiding a person who is too proud to face the reality of his or her own need. If you want to grow in humility, take time to search your soul in the light of the Scriptures. What you find there will humble you.

Another step in Bernard's list is boasting. See if you recognize any of these symptoms of a presumptuous person, as described by Bernard:

> He airs his ideas in a loud and lofty tone. He interrupts his questioner, and he gives answers before he is asked. He asks questions and also supplies the answer. He cuts in on the person talking without allowing him to finish speaking. . . . He gives masses of information all to no purpose. He does not want to teach you, or to learn from you the things he does not know, he just wants you to know the extent of his own learning.[2]

Later, Bernard described the audacity of the proud person, and again, his penetrating description seems strangely familiar. "He reopens discussions of subjects which have been settled, and he goes over work that has been completed. He thinks that nothing is properly organized or correctly carried out unless he has organized or executed it himself."

I have found it helpful to try and trace that road in the opposite direction: Humility would be seen in accepting decisions that have already been made, rejoicing in the good work of other people, and in trusting others to organize what has been given to them without interfering. Humility is very practical.

COURAGE IN THE HOUSE OF LORDS

Humility is a special challenge for people who have enjoyed great success. It is hard to be humble if you have been blessed with outstanding gifts, have built a successful business, or have worked your way up a career ladder. It is hard to be humble if you are good at sports or music, or if your children are unusually talented.

Humility is also a challenge for people with high moral principles, and that's why it's such a big issue for Christians. A member of the British House of Lords known as Lord Longford wrote an outstanding book on this subject, simply entitled *Humility*.

Longford was a highly successful politician and a man of deep moral principle. The most memorable moment of his life came in 1967, when a bill was brought before the House of Lords to legalize abortion in Britain. Lord Longford stepped down from his position as leader in the House of Lords in order to speak against the bill. It was an act of great courage and a moment of high drama.

For many people, Longford was a hero who was ready to stand up for what was right irrespective of the cost, and to place his moral conscience above considerations of his career or his political party. But reflecting on that great moment, Longford himself had another perspective:

The action I am proudest of during those years was leaving the Leader's seat in the House of Lords and speaking from a back bench against the Abortion Bill—an unprecedented step for someone in my position. Here, if anywhere, in my career, I like to think, was boldness but if I can judge by my internal condition at the time, precious little humility.[3]

I find that a deeply searching confession. Humility is hard for successful people with high moral principles.

Christians need to listen to the criticisms of those who do not like us, and one of these criticisms is that we are arrogant and self-righteous. That is a terrible accusation because the very essence of the Christian faith is that we have come to see our desperate need of the mercy of God. The whole point of the gospel is that it excludes boasting.

Jesus told a story about two men who went into the temple to pray. One was a Pharisee. He had the highest moral principles, but he did not have humility. The other was a publican. His life had been a moral mess, but he saw that he needed the mercy of God, and Jesus said that this man, not the other, went home justified. (See Luke 18:10–14.) Humility is the first sign that a person has understood the gospel. It is crucial for our own spiritual lives and for our witness to the world.

RELEASE FROM
THE TYRANNY OF SELF

Humility is not about denying your gifts or exaggerating your faults. There is absolutely no value in a good-looking person trying to believe that he or she is ugly, or in an intelligent person trying to believe that he or she is stupid. That's not humility—it's just dishonesty. It is a flight from truth, and it dishonors God who gave these gifts of body or mind in the first place.

Don't talk down what God has enabled you to do. If someone compliments you on a job well done, accept the compliment. Don't tie your mind in knots by suggesting that something good was of no value. That can be a subtle form of self-centeredness, as can the self-deprecating complaints of a person who exaggerates his or her own faults and bemoans their own lack of ability or appeal. Low self-image can be a manifestation of pride as much as inflated self-image because both involve a preoccupation with self.

Humility, in the first instance, is a wonderful release from the tyranny of self. Jesus said, "If anyone would come after me, he must deny himself" (Matthew 16:24). He does not call you to deny your gifts and abilities, or to pretend that what you do is of no value. The calling is to "deny yourself," that is, to break the power of your consuming interest in yourself.

The letter "I" lies at the heart of "pride," and the cross represents the letter "I" cancelled out. It is through the cross that you will find the power to live a God-centered life in a self-centered world.

REFLECTING THE BEAUTY OF JESUS

The word *humility* seems to be in the wrong company. It gets associated with unattractive words like *humiliated* or *humbled,* which suggest being brought down to size, or being embarrassed by failure, and that's hardly attractive. Christians often associate humility with sin: The reason that I should be humble is that I am a sinner and therefore I have nothing to be proud about.

But Jesus had no sin, and He is our model of humility. He has all the gifts and is worthy of the highest praise, and yet He is humble. Andrew Murray has captured the attractiveness of humility in these words, "If humility is to be our *joy*—we must see that it is not only the mark of shame because of sin, but, apart from all sin, humility is being clothed upon with the very beauty and blessedness of heaven and of Jesus."[4]

That insight has opened up a new world for me. Humility is beautiful. It is powerfully attractive. The glory of Jesus is seen in His humility, as He takes the form of a servant and calls us to reflect His glory as we humble ourselves and follow His example in serving others.

Humility, like a precious stone, is beautiful, valuable, and worth many sacrifices to obtain. Imagine being released from the tyranny of preoccupation with yourself. Imagine the beauty of Jesus being seen in you. Far from the world of failure and shame, humility, properly understood, is powerfully attractive.

WHEN GOD IS AGAINST US

God opposes the proud. (VERSE 5)

Pride, by contrast, is ugly. It was the first movement of Satan's soul as he sought to take the place of God, and the first movement of Eve's soul when he seduced her in the garden with the suggestion that she could be like God. Pride is always destructive. There is nothing remotely attractive about it.

Peter tells us that God opposes the proud. That's strong language and it's worth taking a moment to let these words sink in. God actively resists proud people. He stands in their way, and eventually He will bring what the proud person is trying to do to nothing.

Remember that Peter is writing to Christian believers. He is making it clear that it is possible to throw all the effort of your life into serving Christ and yet to achieve nothing of lasting significance. If God opposes me, or stands in the way of what I seek to do in His name, then it will all come to nothing. The apostle Paul talks about the same thing using a vivid picture when he describes the Last Day when all of our ministry and service will be tested by fire. Some of our work will be like gold, silver, and precious stones. It will survive the test of fire. But some of it will be like wood, hay, and stubble. The test of fire will consume it so that nothing of value remains (1 Corinthians 3:12–15).

Throughout our study of 1 Peter we have been discovering God's great purpose for our lives. We have seen how He can use us to touch the lives of others with His grace. But Peter wants us to know that none of this can happen if pride gets in the way.

GOOD SOIL
FOR SPIRITUAL GROWTH

God . . . gives grace to the humble. (VERSE 5)

The prospect of God opposing us gives good reason to shun pride, but the promise of God's grace is an even better reason for pursuing humility. We sometimes use the expression "Money makes money." You have to have some before you can make some. Well, it's the same principle here: Humility is a grace that attracts more grace.

Pride closes the door to spiritual growth, but humility opens the door of your life to more of God's grace. Pause for a moment to ponder this promise and let it sink in. God gives grace to the humble.

If you pursue humility, you will grow as a Christian. The fruit of the Spirit grows in the soil of humility. As you pursue humility, you will find yourself growing in patience, gentleness, love, and self-control. You will also experience a new and increasing level of peace, yet another benefit of humility to which Peter draws our attention.

RELEASE FROM ANXIETY

Humble yourselves, therefore, under God's mighty hand. . . . Cast all your anxiety on him because he cares for you. (VERSES 6–7)

Have you ever thought about the connection between pride and worry? The proud person feels that he or she is in control, and that's where worry begins. Pride will always leave you anxious.

Since pride is a root of worry, humility is a path to peace. Conquering anxiety begins by dealing with pride. You cannot add an inch to your height or an hour to your life by worrying about it. Pride reckons that what happens is in your hands, but the reality is that what happens to you is ultimately in the hand of God.

Humility puts you in the position where you are able to roll the burden of your worries onto God. Peter made the connection clear by bringing humility and freedom from anxiety together in one sentence. Literally translated, Peter said, "Humble yourselves . . . casting all your anxieties on him for he cares for you."

Peace begins when you humble yourself. You are not in control of what happens in your family, your work, or your church. But God is, and He cares for you. Grasping that reality will put you in a position to prevail in your battle with anxiety.

PRACTICAL STRATEGIES
FOR CULTIVATING HUMILITY

Once you have seen the attraction and value of humility, you will want to pursue it, and Peter tells you how. Humility doesn't just happen. It is cultivated by intentional choices. Choose to "clothe yourselves with humility" and "humble yourselves" (verses 5–6).

Think about your morning routine. The alarm goes off; you roll out of bed and stagger toward the shower. You clean your teeth and head toward the closet, where you face the first of the day's great choices: "What am I going to wear?"

That's exactly how you should think about humility. In the same way as you choose your clothes in the morning, God calls you to choose the attitude of mind and heart that you will wear in the world each day. Clothe yourself with humility. It's an intentional choice to be made on a daily basis.

Clothing is your most visible personal statement. It is the first thing that another person sees, and it forms the impression you choose to convey. Let humility be your personal statement. Let it be something that others see in you.

Think about the way you choose the clothes you will wear. You want them to be suitable. You will consider the weather—is it warm or cold outside?

You will think about what you have to do—are you working in the yard or are you attending a wedding?—then you will choose suitable clothes.

Humility is always the suitable clothing for a follower of Christ. A proud Christian would be as ridiculous as a man in an overcoat in the height of summer, or a woman wearing gardening clothes at a wedding reception.

Imagine a closet filled with clothes that you could choose to wear as you move into a new day. They include self-importance, self-interest, and self-promotion, and you have to decide what you are going to wear. Peter urges you to leave these rags in the closet and to clothe yourself in humility.

Humility is not something that happens to you; it is a choice that God calls you to make. So don't wait for God to make you humble. Cultivate humility. Make it your intentional approach to the whole of life.

GAZING AT THE GRACE OF GOD

I love the fact that it is Peter who writes with such winsome power about the grace of humility. He had learned it from his own experience, which must have come to mind when he described himself as "a witness of Christ's sufferings" (verse 1).

Peter could not have written these words without remembering his greatest moment of failure. When Jesus was arrested, Peter denied him three times, and in recalling that scene, Peter is saying, "I know my own failures." But this was not an exercise in self-condemnation. When Peter looked back, he could see how far he had come by the grace of God, and that cultivates humility.

Never lose sight of what God's grace has done in your life. It's easy to forget as you move on in your Christian experience, and that is why the New Testament repeatedly reminds Christian believers of our spiritual position before Christ broke into our lives.

Remembering your past sins and failures is both dangerous and valuable. The danger is that you might move into a gloomy world of regret and condemnation. That is precisely what Christ died to free you from, so don't go there.

When your past sins and failures come to mind, seize the opportunity to give thanks to God for His grace that intercepted your life. Look back and trace how far God's grace has brought you, and you will grow in humility.

And then look forward. That's what Peter did. When he faced the memory of his failure, he turned to consider his future, and alongside the description of himself as "a witness of Christ's sufferings," he says "and one who also will share in the glory to be revealed."

Contemplating the grace and mercy of God is like gazing at the Grand Canyon, or the Swiss Alps. You don't come away from such grandeur filled with a sense of your own importance; you come away thrilled by the glimpse of something far greater than yourself.

What God is doing in you now is only a small sample of what He will do when Jesus Christ is revealed. You will share in His glory. When you see Him, you will be like Him, and all of this is a free gift that flows from God's grace to you in Jesus.

NOTES

1. Bernard of Clairvaux, *The Twelve Steps of Humility and Pride*, ed. Halcyon C. Backhouse (London: Hodder & Stoughton, 1985), 57.

2. Ibid., 58.

3. Frank Pakenham, Earl of Longford, *Humility* (London: Collins, 1969), 30.

4. Andrew Murray, *Humility* (Fort Washington, Pa.: Christian Literature Crusade, 1997), 9.

DISCOVER. . .

. . . why Christ wants you to be part of His church.

. . . how to pray for Christian leaders.

. . . a glimpse of your future life with Christ.

10
New Destiny
1 Peter 5:1–4, 8–14

A few days ago, I met with a man who, like me, was born in Scotland and is now living in America. It was evident from our conversation that he was a believer and we held many things in common. He knew people and places in Scotland that were familiar to me, and although we had never met before, we soon found ourselves tapping into a fund of mutual memories.

Sometime into the conversation, it seemed natural to ask him where he worshiped. "Oh," he said, "I've lost interest in organized religion." Then he began to relate a sad story of various disappointments he had experienced in church. The heart of what he was saying was simple: The church isn't what it ought to be. So he had opted to become a lone believer, with a personal faith. There are many like him.

Our last key for unlocking the Christian life involves the church and her destiny. In this chapter, we're going to open up a dimension of the Christian life that many in our highly individualistic society long to experience, but struggle to grasp.

You can follow the path of Buddhism or Hinduism in private. But Christ calls us to follow Him together. Each of us must make a personal journey to the cross, but at the cross we meet together. When you came to Christ, you became part of a community with a purpose and a destiny, and its name is the church.

THE FLOCK OF GOD

To the elders among you, I appeal as a fellow elder. . . . Be shepherds of God's flock that is under your care. (1 PETER 5:1–2)

After years of hyper individualism and consumerism, a new generation is searching for authentic community. This hunger represents a great opportunity for the church. A church is simply a community of believers in one locality, drawn together by their common experience of the grace of God in Jesus Christ with the purpose of honoring and serving Him.

The Bible uses many pictures to describe the church. God's people are like a body in which each member has a role to play. They are like a bride in love with Christ and preparing for the wedding day. They are an army prepared for battle against the spiritual forces of evil at work in our world.

But one of the oldest and most beautiful pictures of God's people is the image of sheep nurtured by a shepherd. God's purpose is not just that you would belong to Jesus, but also that you would be part of an identifiable flock of God's sheep, under the care of trusted spiritual leaders.

HELPING SICK SHEEP

I've found it helpful to remember that, like sheep, many of us are stubborn and weak; the church flock will always reflect the struggles of the individuals who make it up. Think about your struggles with greed, pride, and insensitivity: expect to see them all in the church.

Some people look at the church and don't like what they see. But if you are honest, you would admit that when you look in the mirror, you have the same problem.

If I fight ongoing battles with selfishness, insensitivity, pride, and greed in my own life, then I have to expect that others around me will be in precisely the same position. So in our search for community, let's be realistic. The Christian church is not a club for nearly perfect saints. It is a hospital for recovering sinners, and it is filled with people at all stages of the recovery process.

Further, if the church is to be true to its calling, it must embrace difficult people who would be shunned elsewhere. I think of a lady who throughout her life attended the church I pastored in London. She had many problems and caused many more. She would often write anonymous letters, sometimes suggesting that she should be invited to sing a solo on Sunday. She had to be confronted after she was seen taking money from the offering plate, and we had difficulties more than once when she invited people from the church to join her at a restaurant for lunch then, having conveniently forgotten her handbag, invited them to pay!

Thinking back, I don't think that there was ever a year when the leaders of the church did not have to deal with some problem that arose because of this lady, and as she became older, it got worse. Life would have been much easier if we had thrown her out, but would that have been the right thing for the church to do?

This lady did not have a single living relative. If it had not been for the faithful kindness of a few people in the church, she would have been completely isolated in an institution without a friend in the world.

None of the secular guilds or clubs in the community would put up with her. Only the church had the grace and the patience to love and forgive and confront, and to persevere.

It is easy to talk about caring for the lost person outside the church. But the first test of authenticity is whether we care about the difficult person inside the church. It's good to remember that if you come across somebody in the church who is rude, insensitive, or just plain eccentric. Remember that they are like sheep who need a shepherd.

I have a picture in my mind of a believer standing in heaven and proclaiming his love for Jesus. Christ turns to him and says, "If you love Me, why did you not care about the body of which I am the head?"

The believer looks up into the face of Christ and says, "Lord, You are wonderful but the church is sometimes very unattractive."

"If you knew anything about Me," Christ says, "you would have learned to love what is sometimes unattractive."

It's not difficult to choose a few friends who are all like-minded and create a small group around a common interest. But authentic community involves more than that. The first community God places us in is called the family. None of us chose our family. Your family are the people God has placed around you. They may be wonderful, they may be terrible, or they may be a mixture of the two, but they are the people God has placed next to you, and the way you interact with them will play a significant role in the shaping of your character.

The church is the family of God. It is a community of people gathered by God, not a clique chosen by us, and the way that you relate to your church family will play a large part in shaping the person you become.

PRAYERS AND PITFALLS
FOR CHRISTIAN LEADERS

Be shepherds of God's flock that is under your care, serving as overseers—not because you must, but because you are willing, as God wants you to be. (VERSE 2)

A community must have leaders, and Peter has some words of encouragement for elders who are given that responsibility in the church. From the earliest days, the church recognized spiritual leaders. They were either elected or appointed, and they were given the responsibility of shepherding God's flock.

The flock belongs to Jesus Christ. He is the Chief Shepherd (5:4; see also 2:25), and the elders are called to serve Him by caring for and overseeing the flock that He has put under their care.

Most of us live a long way from an animal farm, but we know what shepherds do: They guard the sheep against danger, lead the sheep to places where they find pasture, and search for sheep who get lost or have become injured.

One of the great blessings of the church is that you come into a relationship with other people who care about your spiritual well-being. This is where you are fed and nourished, and it is the responsibility of spiritual leaders to make sure that it is so. The names of spiritual leaders vary in different churches, but the principle is the same: The church is to recognize spiritually mature people to give oversight to the flock of God.

Spiritual leadership is a dangerous business. Satan knows that he can do great damage to God's flock if he can subvert one of the shepherds. It is important to know how this sometimes happens so that you can pray intelligently for the leaders of your church.

We have already seen that the battle against sin lasts a lifetime, so it should not surprise you to learn that even mature Christians have their struggles. Pastors, elders, and missionaries need your prayers, and Peter identifies three areas in which leaders are especially vulnerable.

The first is loss of vision. Peter urges Christian leaders to serve "not because you must, but because you are willing, as God wants you to be" (verse 2). Pastors and missionaries usually launch out into ministry with a great passion to serve Christ; but after five, ten, or twenty years, ministry can easily become a duty that needs to be done. The routine of meetings to attend, sermons to prepare, and counseling sessions to continue can quickly erode a leader's vision. Peter urges Christian leaders to move ministry beyond the level of duty and to avoid the pitfall of laziness. So when you pray for your pastor, leaders, or missionaries, pray that they will be motivated. Pray that their work will not be a duty but a delight.

A second common temptation for Christian leaders revolves around money. Peter urges Christian leaders not to be "greedy for money, but eager to serve" (verse 2). From the earliest times, the church supported pastors and missionaries so that they could give themselves fully to the work of ministry. Living from the support that others are able to give is a privilege, but it can also bring its pressures.

Before I became a pastor, a close friend said to me, "Colin, you will need to decide before you go into ministry how important money is for you. And if you don't do that now, it will haunt you all of your life." I'm glad he confronted me with that challenge. Most people who serve as missionaries or in full-time ministry have to grapple with this issue.

Christ wants us to be eager to serve. Those who go into ministry with the question "What can I get out of it?" will not last long. We must offer ourselves to Christ and give ourselves to ministry. We must ask, "What can I put into it?" So pray that Christian leaders will find great reward in the fruitfulness of their work and that they will be content.

A third pitfall involves the abuse of power. Peter warns Christian leaders against "lording it over those entrusted to you" and urges them to lead by "being examples to the flock" (verse 3).

"Lording it over the flock" means telling everybody else what to do, when you don't do it yourself, and of course that's hypocrisy. Christian leaders have a special responsibility here. There is no greater stumbling block to a church than leaders who say one thing in public and do something else in private.

The greatest challenge for every missionary, pastor, elder, Sunday school teacher, and board member is to practice what we preach. So pray that those who are called to leadership will be authentic. Where the church has leaders who are strongly motivated, deeply contented, and truly authentic, then God's people will be blessed.

WATCH OUT FOR THE LIONS

Be self-controlled and alert. Your enemy the devil prowls around like a roaring lion looking for someone to devour. (VERSE 8)

If Satan can't overpower the shepherds, he will come looking for the sheep, and so having explained some ways in which our enemy seeks to subvert Christian leaders, Peter goes on to warn the whole church about the ferocity of the Devil.

When Peter speaks about "your enemy," he is speaking to the whole community of believers. The Devil is the enemy of the whole church, and one of his primary strategies is to pick off vulnerable sheep who become isolated from the flock.

Imagine you and I are part of a group of one hundred people on safari. We are organized in groups of ten, and every time we get on the bus, we check to make sure that everybody is there. Suppose when we are out in the open, someone from your group wanders off on her own. Someone needs to go and bring her back. The group will take action, not because we are control freaks but because we all know the danger: There are lions out there!

That's the picture Peter is using here. The church is a community of believers making a journey through life together. We are the flock of God, and we have a dangerous enemy who is prowling around looking to pick off God's people, one by one.

Satan is constantly looking out for believers who become isolated, discouraged, and alienated from the rest of the flock. That's why we all need to be self-controlled and alert. It's not just that you need to watch out for yourself; we all need to watch out for each other. Be alert to those God has placed next to you who may be struggling and in spiritual danger, and keep close to other believers so that you do not become isolated yourself.

THE CROWN OF GLORY

When the Chief Shepherd appears, you will receive the crown of glory that will never fade away. (VERSE 4)

A crown of glory is promised not just for elders, but for all those who serve Christ faithfully. Leadership is just one spiritual gift, and the church functions effectively when all of us use the gifts God has given to serve Him.

When Peter talks about a crown, he is talking about a symbol of honor. I can't imagine wanting to spend eternity with a lump of gold on my head, so I am thankful that Peter does not say we will receive a crown of gold, but a crown of glory.

In the Old Testament, God said, "Those who honor me I will honor" (1 Samuel 2:30). And I think that is the best way to understand what Peter is saying here: The one who serves well will be highly honored in God's presence for all eternity, and that honor will never fade away.

Peter returns to this theme where he speaks about "The God of all grace, who called you to his eternal glory" (1 Peter 5:10). *Glory* is the word we use to describe the brightness and splendor of God's immediate presence. When His ultimate purpose is fulfilled, you will share His glory, and His glory will be seen in you.

DIMENSIONS OF GLORY

It's worth taking time to think about your destiny. The glory of heaven is beyond your ability to grasp, but the Bible gives enough information to ignite your imagination as you contemplate the life you will soon enjoy. Here are ten dimensions of your future life in the presence of God.

1. *Capacity.* When you are in glory, you will be everything that God created you to be. Your body will be transformed. Your mind will be renewed. Your memories will be healed. Your entire soul will be redeemed, and you will have the capacity to live as you always

wished you could. Your love for God and for other people will be pure and complete. Your desires will be completely aligned with the purposes of God.

2. *Community.* When you are in glory, you will revel in the joy of deep and lasting relationships. In the book of Revelation, John describes his vision of a Holy City: a vast crowd of people, living in joyful community together. Think about the deepest and most intimate relationship of your life, or if that is hard for you, think about the dream within your heart of what that may be like. That joy is a pointer to what lies ahead for you in glory.

3. *Clarity.* When you are in glory, you will see everything clearly. "Now we see but a poor reflection as in a mirror; then we shall see face to face" (1 Corinthians 13:12). Mysteries that you cannot begin to understand now will be made known to you, and in the light of that knowledge, God will wipe away all tears from your eyes.

4. *Beauty.* When you are in glory, you will savor the beauty of God's redeemed creation. Think of the beauty of this world. Even under the curse of sin, we enjoy the marvels of God's creation. But God has said, "I will make everything new." There will be a new heaven and a new earth, and your redeemed senses will be filled with the beauty of God's restored creation.

5. *Variety.* When you are in glory, you will enjoy the endless variety of pleasures that God has prepared for His people. You will never be bored. You will never find yourself saying, "Been there, done that." Right now, we are limited by time and space, but in eternity these limitations will be removed, and when that happens in God's new creation, an unimaginable variety of experiences will be opened up for you. Life will be filled with pleasures from God's hand and they will always be new (Psalm 16:11).

6. *Safety.* When you are in glory, you will be completely secure. There will be no enemies or threats, no dangers or accidents. You will be able to savor the joys of life without fear.

7. *Creativity.* When you are in glory, you will find full expression for your creativity. God is the Creator, and your creativity is a reflection of His image. Think of what human creativity can accomplish in this fallen world through art and music, and you have a small sample of what we will explore and enjoy together when the eternal glory of the Creator rests on all His people working in harmony together.

8. *Intimacy.* When you are in glory, you will be fully known, and you will have no shame. Even sexual intimacy will be transcended as you discover what it is to know the full depths of another person and to be known and understood and accepted fully and completely.

9. *Immediacy.* When you are in glory, you will enjoy the immediate, joyful, and visible presence of the Lord Jesus Christ. You will see face-to-face the one you love heart-to-heart. Christ will personally lead you into the joys of eternal life and His presence will be your greatest joy.

10. *Eternity.* When you are in glory, you will know joy without interruption is a life that will never end. This is your destiny.

FROM HERE TO ETERNITY

The God of all grace, who called you to his eternal glory in Christ, after you have suffered a little while, will himself restore you and make you strong, firm and steadfast. To him be the power for ever and ever. Amen. (VERSES 10–11)

It's good to take time to strengthen your grip on eternity, but you still have to face the challenges of your life right now. Peter wants you to know that God will bring you through everything you face from here to eternity.

You may suffer for a while, but God will never let you go. He is able to restore your soul, and He will bring you through what may seem overwhelming to you now. That's a great truth to hold on to when you feel that you are losing your grip. The greatest trials of your life are passages in your journey to the eternal glory to which you have been called.

That confidence will sustain you in the worst of times. God has called you to His glory. This is your destiny. Whatever the difficulties of your life, you know that this will be the outcome, and when you know the destination, you will not mind the journey.

Christ is able to bring you to glory and He will do it. And when you grasp that, you will want to join Peter in his affirmation of praise:

"To Him be the power forever and ever. Amen."

Study Guide

INTRODUCTION

This study guide will help you in personal study and especially in a discussion group, as you apply what you have learned. I am grateful to my colleague Tim Augustyn for his excellent work in preparing this material.

The study is designed for use in ten sessions. Read one chapter of this book and then prepare your answers to the questions that follow before your small group meeting. Notice that each numbered item in a chapter begins with an excerpt from the main text that reviews a key argument or truth.

We encourage small groups to begin each session by reading the relevant verses from 1 Peter. Then ask for God's blessing on your time together, and launch into the questions.

Our prayer is that this material will help you to grasp what God has done for you in Christ and to discover the joy of pursuing the Christian life.

NEW BIRTH
Chapter One

1. "Praise be to the God and Father of our Lord Jesus Christ! In his great mercy he has given us *new birth* into a living hope through the resurrection of Jesus Christ from the dead" (1 Peter 1:3; all Scripture italics added). There is a great deal of confusion over what is meant by the phrase "born again." People ask, "Are you a born-again Christian?" as if this was one brand among many.

   When you initially heard of a "born-again" Christian, what was your impression? Was it an attractive or unattractive term? Why?

   _____

   _____

   _____

   Now that you know what the Bible means by being "born again," how would you respond to someone who asks, "Are you a born-again Christian?"

   _____

   _____

   _____

2. God never intended you to spend your life trying to be like somebody else. Every person reflects a unique angle of the glory of God. In the new birth, God takes your unique individuality and gives you a new disposition so that you can begin to live for His glory.

Ask two people who know you well (a family member, coworker, or friend) to try and describe what makes you uniquely you. Write down anything that resonates with you or surprises you.

Person #1 (name):   *characteristics:*

_____

_____

_____

Person #2 (name):   *characteristics:*

_____

_____

_____

Which of these characteristics are you tempted to smooth out in order to "fit in" at church? Why?

_____

_____

_____

3. I can't recall anything about my natural birth, but that does not cause me to doubt that I exist! The evidence that I was born is that I am alive. It's the same with the new birth.

"The evidence that a person has been born again is that they are living the new life." Do you ever have doubts about whether you are truly born again? Put yourself in the role of a crime investigator—what evidence would you use to convict yourself of having new life?

_____

_____

_____

4. "In his *great mercy* he has given us new birth" (1:3). Have you ever wondered why God moved in *your* life to bring you to faith? After all, there are millions of people who have never come to faith in Christ. When I think about the fact that some of my neighbors, family, and friends have never experienced the new birth, it leaves me asking the question "Why me?"

"The only answer to that question is the mercy of God. Birth is something that happens to you. You do not contribute to it. God did not breathe new life into you because you were a better person or more sincere, or more worthy than your unbelieving neighbors or friends." Rewrite the Bible's answer to the question "why me?" in your own words:

_____

_____

_____

_____

5. "Through faith *[you] are shielded by God's* power until the coming of the salvation that is ready to be revealed in the last time" (1:5). I've met many Christians who believe God has an inheritance for them in heaven, but they sometimes wonder if they will arrive in heaven to receive it. God wants you to know that your salvation does not depend on your ability to hold on to Christ, but on Christ's ability to hold on to you. That's the basis of Christian confidence or assurance.

How confident are you that you will arrive in heaven to receive your inheritance? Circle your answer.

←————————————————————————————————→

fearful   inconsistent   confident

Trace your level of confidence back to the object of your faith. What connection do you see?

_____

_____

_____

_____

6. "For a little while you may have had to suffer grief in *all kinds of trials.* These *have come so that your faith . . . may be proved genuine*" (1:6–7). How can you know that your faith is authentic? How do you know that it is not a passing phase? Peter has the answer. When you suffer grief in all kinds of trials, you will have all the evidence you need that your faith is authentic. Here's why: *If your faith were just a human decision or a passing phase, then as soon as you began to suffer, you would renounce your faith, and turn away from God.*

Identify one trial you have faced as a Christian. How did you respond? How did this trial affect your faith? Reflect on the evidence God has provided that your faith is authentic and not just a human decision or a passing phase.

trial _____

_____

your response _____

_____

your faith _____

_____

7. Realize what God has done for you in Jesus Christ and you will identify with Peter's conclusion: "Though you have not seen him, *you love him;* and even though you do not see him now, *you believe in him and are filled with an inexpressible and glorious joy*" (1:8).

   Write a prayer to God, expressing your love for Him and your trust in Jesus Christ.

   _____

   _____

   _____

   _____

   _____

   _____

   Try to express in words to at least one other Christian friend the joy you have in your heart because of all that God has done for you in Christ.

NEW LIFE
Chapter Two

1. "Just as he who called you is holy, so be holy in all you do; for it is written: 'be holy, because I am holy'" (1 Peter 1:15). If you want a one-word description of the new life God calls us to pursue, that word would be *holiness*.

   Prior to your faith, what would have come to mind when you heard the word *holiness?*

   _____

   _____

   _____

   What is the meaning of the word *holiness?* And what does it mean when God says He is holy? Rewrite the meaning in your own words:

   holiness—_____

   _____

   _____

   God is Holy—_____

   _____

   _____

2. "Therefore, prepare your minds for action. Be self-controlled" (1:13). Holiness isn't something that happens to you. It is something you actively pursue. Your first strategy in this battle with sin is to exercise self-control. Remember, the new life is made possible by the new birth.

Are you struggling with the power of a particular temptation? If so, answer this question as honestly as you can: Do you believe the Holy Spirit lives in you? Explain your answer.

_____

_____

_____

_____

3. "Therefore, prepare your minds for action" (1:13). Sometime soon you will face a situation that will be a temptation to you. . . . Prepare your mind for action. Be self-controlled.

Think of a circumstance in which you have been tempted in the past and you know you will encounter in the future. Your enemy will tell you that you can't control yourself. Don't listen to him. Write down below how you would want to be prepared for this encounter.

_____

_____

_____

_____

4. "Therefore, *rid yourselves* of all malice and all deceit, hypocrisy, envy, and slander of every kind" (2:1; all italics added). Peter is urging us to get rid of all the clutter that would keep us from a life that reflects the holiness of God. And he gives us specific examples of what he has in mind.

Try to give a thumbnail sketch of each example of clutter Peter identifies:

malice— _____

_____

deceit— _____

_____

hypocrisy— _____

_____

envy— _____

_____

slander— _____

_____

How do these things take up "space" in our lives? Take one example from above and describe how getting rid of it might free up more space in your life to reflect the holiness of God.

_____

_____

_____

5. "For you know that it was not with perishable things such as silver or gold that you were redeemed from the empty way of life handed down to you from your forefathers" (1:18).

   How did your "forefathers" try to fill up their empty lives? Think about the various spheres of their lives such as marriage, parenting, work, leisure. What significance did these things hold for them?

   _____

   _____

   _____

What would you be inclined to keep and what would you want God to redeem with His blood?

_____

_____

_____

6. "Now that you have purified yourselves by obeying the truth so that *you have sincere love for your brothers*" (1:22). Holiness is a community project. You cannot be holy on a desert island, because love is the heart of holiness.

Where have you seen the best examples of holiness?

_____

_____

_____

Where have you seen distorted pictures of what holiness is?

_____

_____

_____

Compare and contrast the examples you named above with what you know about Jesus' life:

How are they alike? _____

_____

_____

How are they different? _____

_____

_____

7. "Like newborn babies, *crave pure spiritual milk,* so that by it you may grow up in your salvation" (2:2). You have been born again and your new birth is the beginning of a whole new life in which God calls you to pursue holiness. That means engaging in the fight against sin, living in the light of eternity, and learning to love one another. God has made this life possible for you by the power of His Holy Spirit. It is your responsibility to make sure that this life is nourished as you feed on the Word of God.

Think about the responsibility you and God each have for your new life. Place an *x* on the line in the place that best represents your current view of living the Christian life.

$\longleftarrow$ $\longrightarrow$

all my responsibility   all God's responsibility

What adjustments do you need to make to allow for proper growth of your new life?

_____

_____

_____

_____

NEW PURPOSE
Chapter Three

1. Many people would like to experience the light and hope of God's presence, but they don't know where to find Him. Peter wants us to know that God's presence is found among His people as we worship, live, and serve together.

   Where did you search for light and hope before you began looking among God's people? What attracted you to these particular places?

   _____

   _____

   _____

   What initially attracted you to the church? On a human level, why did you begin looking here?

   _____

   _____

   _____

2. "You also . . . are being built . . . to be a *holy priesthood*, offering spiritual sacrifices acceptable to God through Jesus Christ" (2:5; all italics added). Priests in the Old Testament were the only ones who could enter the inner courts of the temple. You may never have thought of yourself as a priest before, but now that you are a believer in Jesus, that is exactly what you are.

   "The normal assumption in our culture is that anybody can approach God in any way and at any time." Can you think of examples of this assumption in our culture today?

   _____

   _____

   _____

Why do you think this assumption has become "normal" in our culture?

_____

_____

_____

3. Peter describes Jesus as "a stone that causes men to stumble and a rock that makes them fall" (2:8). Two thousand years after His death and resurrection, Jesus still provokes very different reactions.

   What are some reactions you have seen to Jesus?

   _____

   _____

   _____

4. "They stumble because they *disobey* the message" (2:8). Repentance and faith are two sides of the same coin. The one cannot exist without the other.

   What would repentance without faith look like?

   _____

   _____

   _____

   What would faith without repentance look like?

   _____

   _____

   _____

5. "Once you were not a people, but now you are the people of God; once you had not received mercy, but *now you have received mercy*" (2:10). Our shared experience of God's grace is the glue that binds the church together. Each of us has received God's mercy through Jesus. Believers meet on level ground at the cross, and find there a common interest in declaring His praise.

   Describe in your own words why the cross is level ground for all believers.

   _____

   _____

   _____

   _____

6. "Live such good lives among the pagans that, though they accuse you of doing wrong, they may see your good deeds and glorify God on the day he visits us" (2:12). Peter uses the term "pagans" to describe unbelieving people with a generally hostile attitude toward Christ and Christian believers. It would be easy and perhaps natural to feel that deeply resistant people are beyond any hope of salvation. But Peter is not ready to write off even the most hardened pagan. He has a vision of highly resistant people coming to glorify God.

   Think about someone you know who may be deeply resistant to the good news of Jesus. What is your vision for them like?

   $\longleftarrow$ _____ $\longrightarrow$

   beyond hope   unsure   glorify God

   What do you think is the source of Peter's vision for highly resistant people?

   _____

   _____

   _____

   _____

7. "Live such good lives among the pagans that, though they accuse you of doing wrong, they may see your good deeds and glorify God on the day he visits us" (2:12). It's a marvelous vision, but how will highly resistant people ever come to glorify God? The astonishing answer is "through the good lives of Christian believers."

Write the name of someone you know who is a good example of each area below.

a. *acts redemptively* (in situations of division and conflict)

name: _____

b. *prays effectively* (because only God can change the heart)

name: _____

c. *speaks about Jesus with confidence* (so Christ can speak through you)

name: _____

Ask one of these individuals if they would share with you what they have learned in this area.

NEW FREEDOM
Chapter Four

1. By any standards, this was a remarkable change of attitude in a community that had shown itself highly resistant to the gospel. . . . Christian believers had continued to show love, kindness, and mercy toward the village people, and their works had opened the door for their words.

   Where have you seen people who are highly resistant to the gospel undergo a remarkable change of attitude toward it? What do you believe opened the door for this change?

   _____

   _____

   _____

2. *Live as free men,* but do not use your freedom as a cover-up for evil" (1 Peter 2:16; all italics added). Peter's first readers were oppressed by the state, exploited at work, and unhappy at home. Peter tells them to "live as free men!"

   Place an *x* below, indicating your current experience of the Christian life.

   ◄───►

   greatly restricted   real freedom

   Describe one area of your Christian life where you feel either greatly restricted or a new freedom.

   _____

   _____

   _____

   _____

3. "He committed no sin, and no deceit was found in his mouth" (2:22). There are times when telling the truth can get you into serious trouble. When you get into a situation like that, the pressure to use lies and deception to save your own skin can seem almost overwhelming. But Jesus used His freedom to make a different choice.

"Truth is often the first casualty of conflict." When have you given in to overwhelming pressure to use lies or deception to save your own skin?

_____

_____

_____

When have you felt that same pressure but used your freedom to make a different choice?

_____

_____

_____

"In a marketing culture, churches experience increasing pressure to reshape and repackage the gospel to fit with what people want to hear." Have you ever felt pressure to reshape the gospel or reshape what you know to be true about God? What happened?

_____

_____

_____

4. "When they hurled their insults at him, he did not retaliate" (2:23). Perhaps there is a situation in your life where you have been wounded and would love to get even. God may give you that opportunity, and then you will face a choice. . . . The desire for revenge is natural when you are wounded. But freedom means that you do not have to go down that road.

"If your aim is to defeat your enemy, retaliation may be a good option, but if your aim is to win him or her over, you will want to consider a different path." Who do you desire to get even with? Do you believe you are in a position to make another choice? Why or why not?

_____

_____

_____

_____

5. "He entrusted himself to him who judges justly" (2:23). Jesus did not regard the abuse that He suffered as something that should be swept under the carpet and forgotten as if it had never happened. Jesus looked for justice. But He did not pursue it through retaliation, but by trusting the ultimate justice of God the Father.

"God is just. The reason you have a sense of and desire for justice is that God has placed that within your heart." Have you ever felt guilty about desiring justice? Looking back now, do you think it was wrong to have this desire in your heart? Why or why not?

_____

_____

_____

_____

How do you typically approach issues of personal justice?

←——————————————————————→

sweep it under carpet   through retaliation

New Freedom

Practically, what do you think it would look like to trust the ultimate justice of God the Father?

_____

_____

_____

6. "*He himself bore our sins in his body* on the tree so that we might die to sins and live for righteousness" (2:24). If someone wounds you and you choose to retaliate, you reflect the pain that you have experienced back onto them.

"But if you choose not to retaliate, you will find that you absorb the pain into yourself. The pain ends with you because you choose not to pass it on. This is what Jesus did. He chose to act redemptively." Reflect on what this means for you.

_____

_____

_____

7. Are you willing to use your freedom to act redemptively? *Cultivate the habit of applying this principle to every situation of conflict* you face. Choose words that, as best you can tell, are most likely to bring healing.

Write a prayer asking God to help you cultivate the habit of acting redemptively in every situation of conflict you face—beginning this week. Thank Him for freedom in Christ to make this choice.

_____

_____

_____

_____

_____

NEW RELATIONSHIPS
Chapter Five

1. None of them knew anything about the God of the Bible, and in the middle of this crisis they were looking for help. In utter despair the captain of the ship asked Jonah to pray. What a moment!

   "Jonah was surrounded by an entire crew of pagan sailors, and these highly resistant people were asking for prayer!" Have you ever been asked by (or have you ever seen) someone who is highly resistant to the gospel ask another believer to pray? What happened?

   _____

   _____

   _____

2. If we are to fulfill our God-given purpose, we need to be able to pray effectively. For those who are married, this involves nurturing your husband or wife. And for all Christian believers, it means developing healthy relationships within the family of God. Answer the following questions by placing an x on the place that typically reflects you. (If you are unmarried or widowed, answer b only.)

   a. How would your spouse evaluate the way you nurture him or her? (ask your spouse)

   ←—————————————————————————————————→

   ineffectively   inconsistently   effectively

   b. How would you evaluate the health of your relationships within the family of God?

   ←—————————————————————————————————→

   avoid resolving   not close enough   quickly initiate
   conflicts   to have conflicts   conflict resolution

What does your assessment say about your ability to pray effectively? Do you think it is an accurate reflection of your prayer life? Why or why not?

_____

_____

_____

_____

For Women Only

3. "They were submissive to their own husbands, like Sarah who obeyed Abraham and called him her master" (1 Peter 3:5–6). I find it significant that God should identify Sarah as the model for Christian wives.

Reread the following statements from the chapter:

❏ Sarah was a strong-willed woman and she knew how and when to draw the line.

❏ Women who follow the example of Sarah will not give unthinking, slavish obedience to their husbands.

❏ God does not call you to be a cheerleader when your husband is headed in the wrong direction.

❏ She was the voice of God to her husband, and there may be times when God calls you to that ministry too.

❏ The important thing was that Sarah looked up to Abraham and treated him with great respect.

❏ Nobody can play a greater role in enabling your husband to become the man God calls him to be than you.

❏ This lady's faithfulness to her husband will result in a vast crowd of once highly resistant people from every tribe and nation glorifying God for all eternity.

Put a check mark next to the statement that you most desire to be true of you. Why do you desire that?

_____

_____

_____

_____

Put an *x* next to the statement that you find the least attractive to you. Why is it the least attractive?

_____

_____

_____

_____

4. "*Your beauty* should not come from outward adornment, such as braided hair and the wearing of gold jewelry and fine clothes. Instead, it *should be that of your inner self, the unfading beauty of a gentle and quiet spirit*" (3:3). Some women have told me that they have problems with this verse. I can understand why. At first sight it might seem as if Peter is calling wives to a soft-spoken quietness that would be unnatural for a woman whose style is vivacious, determined, or forceful.

"It's helpful to remember that nobody was ever more forceful than Jesus, and yet He was gentle. His strength was under control." Identify one story from the gospels that brings out the trait (His forcefulness or His gentleness) you have the hardest time associating with Jesus. Write the verses down below and why this exemplified the trait for you.

passage: _____ *why?* _____

_____

Reflect on the beauty of this characteristic in Jesus' life.

For Men Only

5. "Husbands, in the same way, be considerate as you live with your wives" (3:7). Your wife has unique struggles, fears, hopes, and dreams.

Think back on recent conversations with your wife—write down anything that comes to mind. Keep your ears open for more insight.

What I believe are my wife's unique:

Struggles	Fears	Hopes	Dreams

"You need to understand them and then let that knowledge shape the way you relate to her." Pray and ask God to show you how He would have these unique things shape the way you relate to her. Write down any thoughts below:

Struggles	Fears	Hopes	Dreams

6. "Husbands . . . treat [your wives] with respect as the weaker partner and as heirs with you of the gracious gift of life, so that nothing will hinder your prayers" (3:7). Treating your wife with respect means honoring her by placing her in a high and exalted position. Your wife has chosen to give herself to you. A large part of her happiness or misery will flow from the way that you treat her.

❑ Regard her as a sacred trust from God.

❑ Honor her with your time and money.

❑ Use your strength to support her and to bless her.

❑ Speak to her in a way that makes her feel that she is honored.

❑ Speak *about* her with praise, so that she will be exalted in the eyes of others.

❑ Be an initiative taker in the interests of your wife and family.

❑ Living a life of love starts with loving those God has placed next to you.

Put a check mark next to the statement that you most desire to be true of you. Why do you desire that?

_____

_____

_____

Put an *x* next to the statement that you find the least attractive to you. Why is it the least attractive?

_____

_____

_____

_____

For Everyone

7. "Finally, *all of you,* live in harmony with one another; be sympathetic, love as brothers, be compassionate and humble" (3:8). Learn to place the tensions, arguments, and disputes that arise in your home and in your church in the larger setting of your life purpose and your usefulness to God.

How effectively are you putting the tensions and disputes in your relationships in perspective?

←——————————————————————————→

I typically don't   I see the connection   I make the connection
see the connection   only *after* things escalate   *before* things escalate

"When you see how much your relationships matter, you will discover a new motivation to reflect the character of Jesus where it matters most." Peter warns us, "The eyes of the Lord are on the righteous and his ears are attentive to their prayer" (3:12). What most needs to change?

_____

_____

_____

_____

If your motivation is low, try to identify why you think this is. Offer this to the group for encouragement and prayer.

_____

_____

_____

NEW CONFIDENCE
Chapter Six

1. God has called us to penetrate our culture with the good news of Jesus Christ, and that means communicating visually and verbally. Highly resistant people need to see God's grace in action before they are ready to hear it explained in words.

   "Demonstrating the gospel in action will not be enough to bring a person to faith in Jesus Christ. The message must be put into words." *Who* put the gospel in words for you? To the best of your memory, *how* did they put the gospel in words?

   _____

   _____

   _____

   _____

   _____

2. Words and pictures are both powerful means of communication. Pictures have the power of impact. Words have the power of content.

   "We live in the age of video and our culture is increasingly formed around the power of images." How do you think this affects our culture's view of God and Christianity? Why?

   _____

   _____

   _____

   _____

What impact do you think this could have on the church over time? Why?

_____

_____

_____

_____

3. "*Always be prepared to give an answer* to everyone who asks you to give the reason for the hope that you have" (1 Peter 3:15; all italics added). A normal Christian life will provoke questions, and when they arise you need to be ready to give an answer. God has spoken to us visually and verbally through the creation and the Scriptures. Our calling is to mirror that pattern of communication so that His truth can be seen in the new creation of our lives and heard in the testimony of our words.

Has anyone ever asked you to give a reason why some aspect of your life is the way it is? What did you say? If not, how will you answer them when they do?

_____

_____

_____

_____

"If what has happened to you is simply an experience, then it is unique to you, and of little value to anyone else. Your hope arises directly from your faith in the risen Lord Jesus Christ, and for this reason the same hope is open to others who put their trust in Him." Reflect on your answer above—how valuable is/was your response to others? Explain.

_____

_____

_____

_____

4. "He was put to death in the body but made alive by the Spirit, through whom also he went and preached to the spirits in prison who disobeyed long ago when God waited patiently in the days of Noah while the ark was being built" (3:18–20). When Noah spoke God's truth, God spoke through him, and when you speak about Jesus, Jesus speaks through you.

Mark the area(s) below you find most intimidating about sharing your faith:

❏ communicating the message   ❏ talking to my own family

❏ the fear of rejection   ❏ how my friends will react

❏ the inconsistencies of my own life   ❏ how I will be labeled

❏ the inability to answer questions   ❏ They might actually be interested!

❏ the time involved   ❏ offending someone

❏ I have no experience   ❏ other _____

"God speaks to people who do not know Him through ordinary Christian believers who are ready to explain that their hope is found in Jesus." Evaluate your fear factor(s) in light of this:

_____

_____

_____

What do you think would further equip you to share the hope you have?

_____

_____

_____

5. "God waited patiently in the days of Noah while the ark was being built. In it only a few people, eight in all, were saved through water" (3:20–21). Of all the characters in human history, God chose Noah as the model for our ministry. That is significant. Noah didn't see great results from his preaching. In fact, at the end of his entire life of ministry only eight people were saved. The important thing about Noah's ministry was that Christ spoke through him.

"Ministry among highly resistant people isn't easy. What matters is not the number of people you lead to Christ, but your faithfulness to Christ in the place where he has set you." Think about where God has set you—what do you think it means to be faithful to Christ there?

_____

_____

_____

_____

6. "In it [the ark] only a few people . . . were saved through water, and *this water symbolizes baptism that now saves you also* . . . It saves you by the resurrection of Jesus Christ, who has gone into heaven and is at God's right hand—with angels, authorities and powers in submission to him" (3:20–22). When you take the step of believing God's promise and putting your trust in Jesus, the Bible describes you as being "in Christ." Just as Noah was brought safely through the first judgment in the ark, so Christ will bring all who are in Him safely through God's final judgment on the world.

Compare in your own words being "in the ark" and being "in Christ":

_____

_____

_____

"Peter is not suggesting that being baptized saves you in itself. Baptism is the sign of a person identifying fully with Jesus, and it is being 'in Christ' that saves you because He has risen and 'has gone into heaven and is at God's right hand, with angels, authorities and powers in submission to Him.'"

Describe the meaning of "baptism" in your own words.

_____

_____

_____

"God was faithful to His promise and brought Noah safely through the flood and into a whole new life. This same God will be faithful to you throughout your life, and then He will bring you safely through the judgment into eternity." What are the implications of God's faithfulness for the way you live your life?

_____

_____

_____

7. "Do not fear what they fear, do not be frightened" (3:14). The rise of terrorism, the spread of cancer, and the uncertainty of the economy have all contributed to a climate of fear. As a Christian believer, you have a unique opportunity to show that knowing Jesus makes it possible to live with confidence in an uncertain world.

   Think about the difference between three approaches to an uncertain world —escapism, positive thinking, and faith in Jesus Christ. How are these approaches different?

   _____

   _____

   _____

   _____

In each approach below, what factors are necessary to continue to live with confidence over the long haul?

escapism: _____

_____

positive thinking: _____

_____

faith in Jesus Christ: _____

_____

NEW URGENCY
Chapter Seven

1. Our aim has been to learn the Christian life from 1 Peter and our commitment has been to follow the teaching of this letter wherever it leads. That has meant taking each paragraph seriously, discovering what it says, seeing how it relates to what has gone before, and applying its teaching to our own lives today.

   Do you feel that you can do this—take each paragraph, discover, see how it relates, and apply the teaching for yourself?

   ←—————————————————————————————————————→

   no   not sure   yes
                    (I haven't tried yet)

   Place a *b* next to the aspect of studying the Bible that you have the "best" handle on and a *p* next to the one you feel you need the most "practice" on. Discuss with your group some ways to practice these things.

   _____ discovering what each paragraph *says*

   _____ seeing how it *relates* to what has gone before

   _____ *applying* its teaching to your own life today

2. "Therefore, since Christ suffered in his body, arm yourselves also with the same attitude, because *he who has suffered in his body is done with sin*" (1 Peter 4:1; all italics added). Many believers look back to a moment when they said a prayer, went forward at a meeting, or were baptized as the moment when their new life began. But you will not be walking with Christ for long before He brings you to a crossroads where it becomes obvious that following Him will cost you something.

When did you first come to a crossroads where you recognized that following Jesus comes with a cost?

_____

_____

_____

"Faith that has low cost usually has low value. . . . When you pay the price, you will find your determination to make a decisive break with sin is strengthened." In your example above, were you willing to pay the price of following Jesus? Comment on how your decision has affected your determination to break with sin.

_____

_____

_____

3. "As a result, he does not live the rest of his earthly life for evil human desires, but rather for the will of God" (4:2). Once you have understood your calling in this world, it will be obvious that you don't have the time to go on messing about with sin.

"The time for making a decisive break with sin is now!" Is there an area in your life in which the Spirit of God has been convicting you of sin? What steps have you taken to *minimize the effects* of or to manage this sin? What costs would be involved in making a *decisive break* with it?

steps? _____

_____

_____

costs? _____

_____

_____

4. "For *you have spent enough time* in the past doing what the pagans choose to do" (4:3). God will give you a limited amount of time to fulfill His purpose in this world. Your time is running out. . . . Many of Peter's first readers could look back on years lived without Christ. These years had been wasted in drunkenness, carousing, and the like. Peter does not remind them of this to build regret, but to *press home the urgency of living wholeheartedly for Christ now.*

Where is your urgency to live wholeheartedly for Christ now?

←—————————————————————————————————→

I'm apathetic	I'm vigilant	I'm paralyzed
and feel like	and feel like	and feel like
"I've got all the time	"I will have	"I don't have
in the world"	just enough time"	enough time"

"You get one chance to do the will of God at high school, one chance to be sold out for Christ at college, one run at raising a godly family, one chance to live out God's call in your career, one run through the dangerous waters of midlife, and one chance to finish strong in your retirement." What purpose of God will you miss out on if you don't serve Christ wholeheartedly now? What are the implications for you? For others?

purpose? _____

_____

for you? _____

_____

for others? _____

_____

5. "They think it strange that you do not plunge with them into the same flood of dissipation, and they heap abuse on you. But *they will have to give account to him who is ready to judge the living and the dead*" (4:4–5). The unbelieving people around you have a limited amount of time before they are called into the presence of God. Their time is running out. The triumph of the gospel is that when you die, you will live, and that is why it is so important that the good news of Jesus should be preached.

Pray about two or three people for whom the Spirit has consistently given you a "burden." Then write their names below.

#1 _____

#2 _____

#3 _____

Ask God what role you can play in their hearing and believing the gospel. After you pray, write down any thoughts that come to mind.

_____

_____

_____

6. "The end of all things is near" (4:7). Nobody knows when Jesus Christ will return but the Scriptures make it clear that this is an event that could happen at any time. . . . The next event on God's calendar is the return of the Lord Jesus Christ in glory. This will not be the end of world history. . . . But it will be the end of our time. God has given us the task of bringing the good news to all people, and we don't have forever to do it.

What do you think is the church's sense of urgency to complete the task today?

←————————————————————————————————→

gone   flagging   very strong

Specifically, what leads you to believe this?

_____

_____

_____

_____

"It is easy for us to settle down into a predictable routine in which church is part of our lives organized for our convenience, and we forget why we are here." When this is true of us, how do you think we can best go about "reminding" one another why we are here?

_____

_____

_____

7. "Each one should use whatever gift he has received to serve others, faithfully administering God's grace in its various forms" (4:10). New Christians often feel that they have little to contribute to ministry. You may think that many years will pass before you are able to be useful to the Lord. Nothing could be further from the truth.

   Ask a Christian or two who know you well how they think you can be useful to the Lord right now. Write down their comments below:

   _____

   _____

   _____

"One of the joys of your Christian life will be to discover the new gifts and abilities that God has given you for ministry and service in His kingdom." What new gifts or abilities have you discovered since becoming a Christian?

_____

_____

_____

_____

"Try to find out what God has equipped you to do. Some simple questions will help you." What do you enjoy doing?

_____

_____

What have you done that seems to have been followed by God's blessing?

_____

_____

_____

"Different people see different needs and that in itself can be a good indicator of the kind of ministry that you can offer to the Lord." What can you see that needs to be done?

_____

_____

_____

NEW REALITY
Chapter Eight

1. "Dear friends, *do not be surprised at the painful trial* you are suffering as though something strange were happening to you" (1 Peter 4:12; all italics added). Sometime in your Christian life you will find yourself living with an unanswered "why?" There's no avoiding this experience. It comes to us all.

   "You throw yourself into following Christ, and then you experience something that just doesn't make sense." Have you ever personally struggled with an unanswered "why?" or known someone who did? What happened?

   _____

   _____

   _____

   _____

2. Painful trials in the Christian life are neither surprising nor unusual. They are normal. Some Christians find this difficult to accept, so it's worth pausing to identify some unrealistic expectations that may exist in your mind or in the minds of other Christians around you. Here are five examples:

   1) Christians always have happy marriages.

   2) Christians no longer struggle with sin, doubt, or fear.

   3) Christians feel pain less because Christ is with them.

   4) Christians should not need medication if they are trusting in Christ.

   5) Christians are safer, healthier, and wealthier than other people.

Which of these expectations do you think is most commonly held by Christians today? What does this imply about who we think God is?

most common: _____ ***implication?*** _____

_____

_____

_____

Which of these expectations do you most find yourself struggling with? What do you think this says or doesn't say about how you see God?

my struggle: _____ ***how I see God?*** _____

_____

_____

_____

3. "Do not be surprised at the painful trial you are suffering, as though something strange were happening to you" (4:12). We usually refer to the sin of our first parents, Adam and Eve, and its disastrous effects as "the Fall." The first sin was the beginning of a pattern of rebellion against God that has run throughout history and continues today.

   "We have been born into a fallen world that suffers all the effects of human rebellion, and painful trials are not strange in a fallen world." How do the people around you make sense of the pain they experience in this life? If you don't know, ask at least two friends or coworkers.

   _____

   _____

   _____

"We don't belong to this world but we do live in it, and so we share in its experience of sickness, loss, tragedy, disaster, and death. Faith in Jesus Christ is not a strategy for avoiding these trials. It is our strength in facing them." *Contrast* the person who puts their faith in Jesus as a strategy to avoid trials and the person whose faith is a strategy for facing them. How does Jesus' life inform this discussion?

strategy to avoid: _____

_____

strategy for facing: _____

_____

Jesus' life: _____

_____

4. *Rejoice that you participate in the sufferings of Christ,* so that you may be over-joyed when his glory is revealed" (4:13). Christian expectations of life in this world should be shaped by the fact that we have chosen to follow a crucified Savior.

"Take a moment to consider Jesus' experience of life in this world, and as you do, think about ways in which you might have shared His experience." Go back now and look at ten of the experiences Jesus had in life. Write below any ways you may have shared His experience.

_____

_____

_____

_____

Learn to shape your expectations by the life and experience of Jesus. Go back and look at the list again. Which experiences on the list go counter to your expectations for your life? Why?

_____

_____

_____

_____

5. "Rejoice that you participate in the sufferings of Christ, *so that you may be overjoyed when his glory is revealed*" (4:13). There is, of course, a magnificent upside to living in this new reality. Those who share in Christ's sufferings will also share in His glory.

"Jesus is risen and exalted at the right hand of the Father, and if you are in Christ this will happen to you!" How does the prospect of sharing in Jesus' glory affect your motivation to share in His sufferings?

←——————————————————————→

the suffering looms so   the weight of glory
large, I can't really see   makes the suffering
the glory look   light and momentary

"Try to think about your trials, frustrations, and disappointments as the great moments of your life. This is where all that God has been doing in your life will be made known." Think back to a trial you have had in the last month. We naturally focus on what we did wrong. Are you able to see how God's work in you was revealed? What do you see?

_____

_____

_____

6. "It is hard for the righteous to be saved" (4:18). The Bible speaks about salvation in three tenses: It is a completed transaction, a continuing process and a future hope. The reality is that you have been saved, you are being saved, and one day you will be saved!

   "Looking back, you have been saved from sin's penalty. A transaction took place when you came to faith in Jesus in which the power of His shed blood was applied to your life. Your sins were forgiven. Your judgment was taken. The deal has been done." What difference would it make if this aspect of your salvation was in the future and not in the past?

   _____

   _____

   _____

7. "It is hard for the righteous to be saved" (4:18). Every Christian knows that the ongoing struggle with sin's power is hard, and that struggle is part of the reality of the Christian life. . . . We are in the process of being saved from sin's power.

   "It is hard for the righteous to be saved, so if you find it easy, there is good reason to question whether you are really a Christian." Authentic faith in Jesus Christ engages our belief (the head), obedience (the will) and love (the heart). Which of the following do you find *most difficult* in the Christian life?

   _____   that God really loves me   _____   prayer

   _____   understanding the Bible   _____   motivation to change

   _____   relating to other Christians _____   other _____

NEW HUMILITY
Chapter Nine

1. Reflect back on your life and the people you have come into contact with. Name one person who you think was notably humble. What do you remember about him or her that you associate with humility?

_____

_____

_____

_____

2. Christians need to listen to the criticisms of those who do not like us, and one of these criticisms is that we are arrogant and self-righteous.

How do you take criticism?

$\longleftarrow \hspace{6cm} \longrightarrow$

| I try to ignore it (hoping it will go away) | I try to take some truth away (and learn from it) | I take it all in (and am devastated by it) |

Try to identify the kernel of truth in this criticism for you personally. What can you learn from it?

_____

_____

_____

3. Low self-image can be a manifestation of pride as much as inflated self-image because both involve a preoccupation with self.

Which of these two do you tend toward when pride is manifesting itself in your life? How are you tempted to justify it in your own mind?

_____

_____

_____

4. Christians often associate humility with sin: The reason that I should be humble is that I am a sinner and therefore I have nothing to be proud about. But Jesus had no sin, and He is our model of humility. . . . Humility is beautiful. It is powerfully attractive. . . . The glory of Jesus is seen in His humility, as He takes the form of a servant

Think about the humility of Jesus in the Incarnation. Describe the glory you see in Him in this act.

_____

_____

_____

_____

5. God opposes the proud but gives grace to the humble" (5:5). That's strong language and it's worth taking a moment to let these words sink in. God actively resists proud people. He stands in their way, and eventually He will bring what the proud person is trying to do to nothing.

"Peter is writing to Christian believers. He is making it clear that it is possible to throw all the effort of your life into serving Christ and yet to achieve nothing of lasting significance." What are the implications of this for evaluating any ministry?

_____

_____

_____

"Pride closes the door to spiritual growth, but humility opens the door of your life to more of God's grace. Pause for a moment to ponder this promise and let it sink in." Look at the contrast in verses five and six. What do you think of when you think of God giving grace to you?

_____

_____

_____

6. "Humble yourselves, therefore, under God's mighty hand. . . . Cast all your anxiety on him because he cares for you" (5:6–7). Peace begins when you humble yourself. You are not in control of what happens in your family, your work, or your church. But God is, and He cares for you.

   Identify a recurring anxiety you are experiencing. How can you apply this to that situation?

_____

_____

_____

7. Remembering your past sins and failures is both dangerous and valuable. The danger is that you might move into a gloomy world of regret and condemnation. That is precisely what Christ died to free you from, so don't go there.

"When your past sins and failures come to mind, seize the opportunity to give thanks to God for His grace that intercepted your life. Look back and trace how far God's grace has brought you, and you will grow in humility." Describe that process in your life.

_____

_____

_____

"And then look forward. . . . What God is doing in you now is only a small sample of what He will do when Jesus Christ is revealed. You will share in His glory." What would you most like God to do in your life between now and the time when Jesus is revealed?

_____

_____

_____

NEW DESTINY
Chapter Ten

1. How would you respond to someone who told you "I've lost interest in organized religion"? What would you most hope for in that conversation?

_____

_____

_____

2. "To the elders among you, I appeal as a fellow elder. . . . Be shepherds of God's flock that is under your care" (1 Peter 5:1–2).

"After years of hyper individualism and consumerism, a new generation is searching for authentic community. This hunger represents a great opportunity for the church." How do you think you and those you are in Christian community with could best serve a generation like this?

_____

_____

_____

"In our search for community let's be realistic. The Christian church is not a club for nearly perfect saints. It is a hospital for recovering sinners, and it is filled with people at all stages of the recovery process." How might this reality affect the way you *search for community?*

_____

_____

_____

"If the church is to be true to its calling it must embrace difficult people who would be shunned elsewhere." Think of a difficult person in the church, someone you avoid because you don't want to "deal with them." How could your Christian community begin embracing them?

_____

_____

_____

3. "*Be shepherds* of God's flock that is under your care, serving as overseers— not because you must, but because you are willing as God wants you to be" (5:2; all italics added). Most of us live a long way from an animal farm, but we know what shepherds do: They guard the sheep against danger, lead the sheep to places where they find pasture, and search for sheep who get lost or have become injured.

In which of these ways have you personally benefited from a spiritual leader? Place an *x* next to any that apply to you.

A spiritual leader has . . .

_____ protected me from danger

_____ led me to spiritual nourishment

_____ brought me back or brought healing to me

Identify up to three specific times when these things happened in your life. Name the spiritual leader and the danger, hunger, or difficulty you have faced.

Name: _____

Issue: _____

_____

Name: _____

Issue: _____

_____

Name: _____

Issue: _____

_____

4. Spiritual leadership is a dangerous business. Satan knows that he can do great damage to God's flock if he can subvert one of the shepherds. It is important to know how this sometimes happens so that you can pray intelligently for the leaders of your church.

"The first is a loss of vision. . . . Pray that they will be motivated. Pray that their work will not be a duty but a delight." Choose one or more spiritual leader(s) and pray this for them by name now.

"A second common temptation for Christian leaders revolves around money. . . . Pray that Christian leaders will find great reward in the fruitfulness of their work and that they will be content." Choose one or more spiritual leader(s) and pray this for them by name now.

"A third pitfall involves the abuse of power. . . . Pray that those who are called to leadership will be authentic." Choose one or more spiritual leader(s) and pray this for them by name now.

5. *"Be self-controlled and alert.* Your enemy the devil prowls around like a roaring lion looking for someone to devour" (5:8). If Satan can't overpower the shepherds, he will come looking for the sheep.

"Satan is constantly looking out for believers who become isolated, discouraged, and alienated from the rest of the flock." Are you aware of a believer who may be in one of the above circumstances? If so, make a phone call and find out how they are doing or stop them at church and encourage them. If the situation looks serious, you may also need to contact a pastor or other spiritual leader to provide additional support.

Name: _____

Plan of action: _____

When? _____

6. "When the Chief Shepherd appears, *you will receive the crown of glory* that will never fade away" (5:4). It's worth taking time to think about your destiny. The glory of heaven is beyond your ability to grasp, but the Bible gives enough information to ignite your imagination as you contemplate the life you will soon enjoy.

Go back and review the ten dimensions of your future life in the presence of God:

Capacity	**Safety**
Community	**Creativity**
Clarity	**Intimacy**
Beauty	**Immediacy**
Variety	**Eternity**

Circle two of the dimensions on the previous page that touch a deep chord in you. What is it about these things that you find so attractive?

_____

_____

What do these tell us about the character of God?

_____

_____

Place an *x* next to two dimensions that have little or no effect on you. Go back and think about them, imagining what it will be like to know these things fully in the presence of God. Write down any new thoughts about the dimension or insights you gain about God.

_____

_____

_____

7. "*The God of all grace,* who called you to his eternal glory in Christ, after you have suffered a little while, *will himself restore you and make you strong, firm and steadfast. To him be the power for ever and ever. Amen*" (5:10–11). God has called you to His glory. That is your destiny. Whatever the difficulties of your life, you know that this will be the outcome, and when you know the destination you will not mind the journey.

Consider the difficulties you are facing (or those you fear) and personalize the following passage with your name and situation. "The God of all grace, who called [your name] to his eternal glory in Christ, after [your name] has [your situation] a little while, will himself restore you and make you strong, firm and steadfast." Now reread the verse with your specific situation inserted. *To Him be the power forever and ever. Amen.*

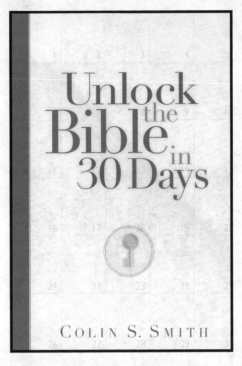

Unlock the Bible in 30 Days

COLIN S. SMITH

If you see the Bible as a series of separate books, you're not just missing the forest for the trees. You're missing out on the greatest story ever told. In just thirty days, Colin Smith will take you on a grand tour of the Scriptures—revealing how the story of God in three persons is interwoven throughout the Bible in one, interlocking narrative. The time has come to unlock this truth for yourself—and this book holds the key.

Unlock the Bible in 30 Days
ISBN: 0-8024-6555-2

For a more in-depth study of the Bible, check out Colin Smith's four-volume masterpiece, *Unlocking the Bible Story*. It will move you past Bible stories to understand the Bible as one story—the glorious, unbroken account of Christ's work to redeem a fallen world.

Unlocking the Bible Story, Volume 1
ISBN: 0-8024-6543-9

Unlocking the Bible Story, Volume 3
ISBN: 0-8024-6545-5

Unlocking the Bible Story, Volume 2
ISBN: 0-8024-6544-7

Unlocking the Bible Story, Volume 4
ISBN: 0-8024-6546-3

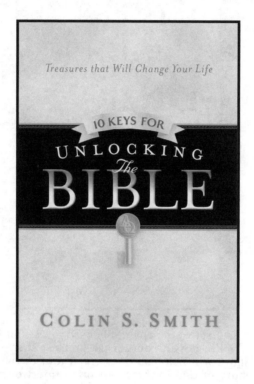

The whole Bible is one story. *10 Keys for Unlocking the Bible* gives you the big picture of the Bible story. Like a high-altitude flight over a range of mountains, this small book will give you a good glimpse of the highest peaks.

10 Keys for Unlocking the Bible
ISBN: 0-8024-6547-1

10 KEYS TO UNLOCK THE CHRISTIAN LIFE TEAM

ACQUIRING EDITOR
William Thrasher

BACK COVER COPY
Anne Perdicaris

COPY EDITOR
Jim Vincent

COVER DESIGN
Smartt Guys

COVER PHOTO
Michael Burke/Index Stock

INTERIOR DESIGN
Paetzold Associates

PRINTING AND BINDING
Versa Press, Inc.

The typeface for the text of this book is
RotisSerif